TORN
Bible

SHARON GREEN

Torn Bible
All Rights Reserved.
Copyright © 2018 Sharon D. Green
v2.0

The opinions expressed in this manuscript are solely the opinions of the author and do not represent the opinions or thoughts of the publisher. The author has represented and warranted full ownership and/or legal right to publish all the materials in this book.

This book may not be reproduced, transmitted, or stored in whole or in part by any means, including graphic, electronic, or mechanical without the express written consent of the publisher except in the case of brief quotations embodied in critic
al articles and reviews.

Sharon Green

ISBN: 978-0-692-07654-5

Cover Photo © 2018 Boree Unlimited. All rights reserved - used with permission.

PRINTED IN THE UNITED STATES OF AMERICA

To everyone who is looking for the words to express the unthinkable and indescribable, to everyone who thinks God has left you when it mattered most, my story is for you. To all of the strong women in my life, including my sister friends, thank you for being patient with me. To my family, thank you for being so loving and devoted to keeping our legacy alive.

To my amazing Mama, thank you so much for keeping and loving me. Thank you so much for being a good sport throughout this process. Telling my story meant telling a part of your story as well. So, thank you! Thank you for allowing me to say what I needed to say. You are the epitome of faith, strength, and unconditional love. I thank God He gave me to you. To God be all the glory!

Table of Contents

Prologue: The Land i

Part 1: Two Cities 1
   1. Lake Providence, LA 3
   2. My Sister: The Strong Quiet Type 8
   3. New Orleans 1975 11
   4. Got Good Religion 17
   5. Don't Tell 23
   6. Secrets and Chaos 28
   7. Deacon Jackson 36

Part 2: Looking For Jesus - Finding Religion 41
   8. Private Schools 42
   9. Rape and Suicide Attempts 46
  10. Marriage and Divorce 54

Part 3: Mental Illness 65
  11. Clinical Depression 66
  12. I Stopped 72
  13. Church Killed Me! 76
  14. Justin 83
  15. Something's on me 89
  16. I heard Him! 98
  17. The Battle for the Mind 106
  18. Family Reunion 110

Part 4: Better Is the End 115
    19. Changing Direction 116
    20. Revelations 122
    21. Confronting Resentment 126
    22. Seeing Why God Blocked him 130
    23. When Deacon Jackson Died, I Saw the Heart of God 132
    24. Layers of Forgiveness 145
    25. Surviving Church 150
    26. Somewhere In the Middle 155
    27. New Life New Eyes 158
    References 165

Prologue: The Land

Lake Providence, Louisiana 1930s

You can get tired of folk. You get tired of being pushed around by them, them being the white folk. You can get so tired until you become emboldened to do something about it. You work so hard to provide for your family on someone else's land, but are still treated like a boy even though you're a man, a real man with a wife and child. You got to ignore it, rise above it and stay focused. That's what Mama told me and what Grandma told her.

Mama's voice grew from a whisper to a strong matter of fact as she proudly explained, "Daddy made sure Mother would never have to worry about anything for as long as she lived. Daddy and Mother lived on a white man's farm and worked his land for room and board. "Your uncle Freddy, the first born, was just a baby and Mother was inside tending to him. Daddy told us that white man came out to him and asked, "Hey boy. Why ain't yo wife out here working this land too?" Daddy responded, "Why your wife not out here working?"

That was the day my Granddaddy, Reverend Freddie Green Sr., decided to get Grandma, who he lovingly called Babe, off the white man's land before he got himself and his family killed. Granddaddy had owned at least three homes as far as I can remember. One he had built, but not live to see completed. He stayed true to his word that Grandma would never have to worry about a thing. Mama said when they were growing up Granddaddy was one of several Baptist preachers fighting against Jim Crow laws and fighting to get the right to vote. He tried organizing to get people to fight back against the KKK and prevent more lynching, but most of the folk were too afraid to ruffle feathers.

Mama said she'd known several young men in town who were victims of lynching and in the same breath thanked God it was never any of her brothers. She said, "Daddy would run down to the local colored hospital to check on other folks' boys who got caught on dark roads and were beaten within an inch of their lives." Granddaddy prayed and stressed to church members, neighbors and friends the need for organizing. I was already well into my adult years by the time I'd heard the whole story about Granddaddy being the local town pastor of three different churches, civil rights activist and sole provider for his family.

I listened attentively as Mama shared stories of her and her sibling's childhood upbringing in Louisiana. She told me the story about my Uncle Bobby. She said, "Bobby used to work for this white man in his barbershop. One day he came home and told Daddy the man hadn't paid him for a day's work. Well, Daddy marched Bobby right back down to that man's shop and demanded he pay him. That man paid him too. Daddy told that man Bobby couldn't work in his shop anymore."

"When they knew Daddy was off working or preaching in Baton Rouge or New Orleans, the KKK would burn crosses in our front yard, but only when he wasn't home because they didn't do anything to us if they knew he would be there."

"Your Granddaddy raised his boys to work hard and learn how to protect themselves and us. Daddy always told us we were just as good as the next person no matter our skin color. He told me and my sisters to be strong and expect nothing but the best. If a man can't take care of his family ain't no need of marrying him."

She shared with me how he'd always tell Grandma, "That girl ain't never gonna get married. She's just too independent and bossy. No indeed, she's not gonna let no man tell her what to do." They laughed about it, knowing he was right. Mama didn't know at the time that Granddaddy was prophesying her future. It wasn't that she wouldn't receive proposals, because she did. Each time her answer had been, "No."

Mama explained, "Men like your Granddaddy came around few and far between. Daddy was a true man of God! He lived what he preached about. He was that man who truly loved his wife, not just privately, but openly so the whole world would know it and see it. Not just the world, but us kids too. Daddy was the kind of man who cared about Mother's feelings, cared about her health, and cared about her as a woman.

Everything we all needed, God allowed him to provide. When he had to whip us, he'd leave home right after. Mother said he left because it hurt his heart to have to whip us and discipline us that way. He brought home gifts, nice suits and big hats to match for Mother each time he came back from his preaching or activist trips, and made sure when she didn't feel well, all of us were quiet so she could rest. He never allowed her to be disrespected by anyone. Now if a man wasn't remotely close to being the kind of man Daddy was, I didn't want to marry him."

I wouldn't know the depth of Mama's words until I'd experienced the kind of men Granddaddy wasn't. Mama and I would come to share many experiences of how we got back to God after years of rips and tears to the heart. For me, it would not only be my heart, but to the body and in the "body."

Mama's words and my Grandparents' example of family and strength would become the foundation of my life, but, not before I died a thousand deaths.

Part 1
Two Cities

New Orleans to Chicago, 1968 - 1986

CHAPTER 1

Lake Providence, LA

November 1986

FOLKS GATHERED IN every room of Grandma's house catching up and eating home cooked food sent over from neighbors up the road and friends several towns over. "Hi you doing, baby? You must be Louise's baby. You all right, shuga?" I didn't know what to say. I didn't know the lady talking to me. Was she a distant relative, neighbor, a pastor's wife from the pastors and ministers alliance Grandma belonged to, or one of her church mother friends? I didn't want to talk with her. I wasn't okay. I was sad, but I didn't want to tell a perfect stranger.

My big sister, Gina and cousin Breanne were in the kitchen, one of them stirring greens and ham hocks with a long two-prong fork, and the other stirred spaghetti in big black pots on the stove with a stainless steel spoon with holes in it. The woman who wanted to be married to one of my uncles, but had to settle for being the spare, walked in.

She and her friend helped themselves to fried chicken, chilled potato salad and homemade biscuits sitting on the kitchen table. She wasn't the type of woman to be discreet. She sashayed her big hips from one end of the table to the other peeking under foil covered trays. No one liked her, but she didn't seem to mind. Gina and Breanne held their composure as long as they could, taking into account that young people should respect older folk. They held out as long as they could until Miss Big Hips said too much and got too comfortable.

It was not a good time for anybody, and certainly not a good time to deal with the likes of her. Grandma had just passed away after suffering an aneurysm of the brain. Grief filled the house like a thick fog. Mama, her sisters, and brothers were in Grandma's bedroom sorting through papers and trying to make funeral arrangements between moments of hugs and tears. My cousins and I made pallets on the family room floor to watch 227, gearing up our vocal chords to sing the theme song. We bobbed our heads to the music and sang in unison.

Our singing was interrupted by yelling coming from the kitchen. Miss Big Hips tried to introduce her friend to Gina and Breanne, calling them her nieces. She'd tried the same thing with us in the family room. My cousins and I just looked at each other, and then back to her. None of us said anything. We were equally irritated that she'd interrupted our television watching.

She walked back into the kitchen and said something to Breanne and Gina. Both of them had their respective utensils in hand along with a few more weapons of destruction raised high and aiming for her, her friend and anybody else who got caught in the cross fire. My cousins and I jumped up and tried to get a glimpse of the action that was more interesting than 227. They'd had enough of her mouth and her disrespect. How dare she come in the house acting like she was a part of the family? I was hoping one them got a hit in before people scurried from all directions of the house to break up the commotion.

My uncle's decision to bring Miss Big Hips to Grandma's house right after her passing was just not right. It was just plain disrespectful. He knew there wouldn't be peace until he took her and her friend to wherever they were staying. That's what my cousins and I overheard one of the great aunts say. I don't remember seeing her or her friend anymore for the duration of our stay in Lake Providence.

I was seventeen and had graduated from high school seven months prior. It was only the second time I'd ever lost someone so close to me. The first was Granddaddy. He'd passed away seven or eight years earlier. He'd moved Grandma back to Lake Providence into the small house right next to great Auntie Honey. I felt sad when he died, but it wasn't like this sadness. This was different. Maybe it was because I was older. Maybe it was because I was too young to go to his funeral. Maybe it was because she was always there, always at home while he went off to work, to preach or fight for civil rights. She was my other mother. She was my Grandma.

It would be the first time I'd feel so nauseated, feel an unfamiliar knotted up stomach and felt tears creeping through closed eyes while I slept. It was grief. It was grief that would be with me for years to come. It was grief that would sneak up on me when I least expected it and at inconvenient moments. It was grief that I didn't know how to express properly, but periodically caused me to behave erratically. It was grief I took out on people who irritated me, people like my sister's husband, who I could see out the corner of my eye when Mama held me outside the church while I cried. "Why is he here? I don't want him here? I hate him," I mumbled into her chest. "It's going to okay," Mama assured me, knowing what I was meaning to say, and wisely ignoring what I did say.

We'd left Grandma's house just an hour before, headed for the little white church with the graveyard in the back. We left Grandma's house, the ranch house Granddaddy had custom built just for her, but didn't live long enough to stay in and enjoy. We left Grandma's house knowing when we returned, the reality of her not coming back would be final. Mama, her sisters and brothers all wore white to match Grandma's white suit. I saw it briefly when I reluctantly glanced toward the front of the church. I hurried to my seat past the line of family and friends waiting to view her.

I didn't want to get a full view of her lying in a casket. I couldn't look at her. From where I sat, I could see her hair that she liked to color dark, because she didn't like gray hair. Mama said I couldn't wear white. I wanted to wear white too. She said the grandchildren weren't wearing white either. It was her attempt to make me feel better. Instead, I wore a navy two-piece jacket and skirt set with a white blouse, white hat and white shoes with bows at the tip.

The service was a blur. There were people crying and sniffing and singing sad songs. During the final viewing, I hurried out of the side door of the church. I still couldn't view her. I didn't want to remember her like that. That woman in that casket wasn't my Grandma. When I thought of Grandma I thought of New Orleans and the narrow two story shot gun house with the front porch. That was home. I thought about the little house in Lake Providence that sat right next to great Auntie Honey's house. As a child, both houses were big. The Barone street house had the big living room that flowed into the family room. The dining room was in the middle and smaller kitchen was in the back of the house. The bedrooms and bathrooms were upstairs, separated by a long hallway.

The Lake Providence house with chickens and turkeys in the back was home too. It's where I played with my cousins. It's where we'd play in the spaces between the houses. It's where we walked up and down the road all day from one ranch house to the trailer home and back to the ranch house. It was the home I ran in and out of because the air was too cold inside and the sun was too hot outside. When I thought of Grandma, I thought of her giving me Father John's, castor oil, or cod liver oil for whatever ailed me. When I thought of Grandma, I thought about her and great Auntie Honey laughing at me because I was being dramatic about not wanting to take medicine or going to bed by myself. In between laughs Auntie Honey would say, "Oh, it ain't that bad." She'd have a piece of peppermint in her hand waiting to give me once I successfully swallowed all of my medicine. Grandma would say, "Stop that squirming and take this medicine." That's what I remembered when I thought of Grandma.

CHAPTER 2

My Sister: The Strong Quiet Type

I DIDN'T SEE Gina cry at Grandma's funeral. I don't remember seeing her cry much at all. She's the strong, quiet type. She's strong willed, not easily swayed and non- emotional. She was newly married to a man I didn't like. I couldn't understand why she would pick him to marry other than him being the father of her baby. She'd had her one and only daughter a few years prior to Grandma's passing.

I wasn't prepared for the nothingness in the months that followed Grandma's passing. I hadn't planned on living in Chicago. I planned on living with Grandma in Louisiana. I planned to go to college, find a job, maybe get married, and live a quiet, peaceful life in the country with her. I didn't plan for anything else. I didn't plan on needing to find a space in time without her. I didn't have a plan of what to do next.

Gina had her own family. It was just Mama and I left at the apartment. I cried often. I didn't tell Mama or Gina. I didn't want them to worry. Mama was dealing with her own grief. So when she asked how I was doing, I lied. "Yes, I'm okay." "No, really, I'm okay with living in Chicago." "I'll be fine with going to the same church." "Yes, I can figure out a college to attend. Yes, I'll find a new career path here."

MY SISTER: THE STRONG QUIET TYPE

I knew Gina wouldn't mind letting me visit with her more often, but I didn't want to intrude on her and her new husband. I knew I could tell her I wasn't okay, but I didn't know how. She wasn't a talker. She was a good listener, but I had no words for her to listen to. Maybe if I just went and sat with her. I would be okay. She always took care of me. I always felt strength around her.

Being six years older, Mama felt at ease knowing she could leave me home with her when I was little. Gina was responsible and dependable. Mama had no worries when she had to go grocery shopping, run errands or work extra jobs because money was tight. When Mama gave instructions to keep the house clean, Gina ordered me out of her way while she cleaned the house spotless. I'd happily go play with dolls or watch television, not wanting to help anyway.

Her temper was famous. If you didn't bother her, she didn't bother you. But if you started it, she'd finish it, like the time I came home from school and saw spots of blood going up the stairs. The further I got to the top of the stairs and into the hallway leading to the bathroom, the more blood there was on the floor. I followed the trail into the bathroom and found her wrapping a towel around her hand that was already blood soaked. "What happened?" I squealed. "I was walking home from school and this guy came out of nowhere and pulled this butcher knife out on me." I gasped, covering my mouth with both hands. I didn't know whether to cry or scream.

My sister calmly continued her account of what happened, ignoring my reaction. "He thought he was going to take my money. Well when he tried to stab me, I grabbed the tip of the knife and it sliced my hand when I pushed him down. After that I ran as fast as I could." "I'm calling Mama," I said running to the kitchen to grab the phone that was on the wall. "I already called her. She's going to take me to the hospital when she gets home." I can't recall her ever panicking about anything. That was the day I thought my big sister was invincible. It was also the day I knew when she lost her temper she was capable of doing major damage.

There were many times I found myself in a headlock or with her hands around my throat for scratching up one of her records, messing with her eight track tapes or giving unwanted opinions about one of her boyfriends. She had no problem locking me out of the bedroom while she talked on the phone with one of her friends about the latest fashion, the latest Earth Wind & Fire record or Parliament's Flashlight that was at the top of the charts.

When it came to protecting and correcting me, she could be counted on to beat up whoever picked on me or checked my pockets for nickels I'd stolen from the babysitter to buy Now and Later and ICEE cups from Ms. Dickson's candy store. It took a long time to get over her telling Mama I took the nickels even though she assured me it was for my own good. She said she didn't want me growing up to be a thief. I said, "But it was just a few nickels." She replied, "It's not just nickels and it's not yours to take. This time it's nickels next time, it'll be more." I got the worse and last whipping of my life. I guess I have Gina to thank for not becoming a common thief. My taking things that didn't belong to me days were over.

CHAPTER 3

New Orleans 1975

I WOKE UP early from a restless night. I'd spent the night with covers over my head lying still in one position, afraid of the boogie man. I slipped out of bed, thankful I hadn't wet myself or the bed out of fear and went to the bathroom to wash my face and brush my teeth. Trying not to wake anyone, I tiptoed down the stairs to the kitchen where I heard Grandma moving about clinging pots and pans. "What are you doing up this early?" Grandma asked. "I don't know," I lied.

Grandma shook her head and continued cracking eggs, knowing exactly why I was up. The tiny kitchen at the back of the house in New Orleans was small compared to the other rooms. It was a large green and white house with old fashion Louisiana character. The smell of coffee gave me a sense of warmth and comfort as I sat at the kitchen table chattering away about the torment I'd endured at the hands of Gina and Auntie Donna the night before. I wanted to taste Grandma's coffee, but I knew she'd say no as she'd done many times before. There was no need for her to remind me that I was only seven years old, too young for coffee.

I told Grandma how Gina and Auntie scared me with their horror stories. I told her how Auntie made me go upstairs to bed by myself in the dark. The sight of tears running down my face and me shaking in my princess house slippers sent them into uncontrollable laughter. I told her how Auntie scolded me while still laughing in her New Orleans twang, "Girl go on upstairs and go to bed. You so scary. Don't nobody want you." "It wasn't funny," I whined to Grandma. The thought of me walking up those stairs that squeaked and walking down that dark, narrow hallway to the bedroom by myself sent me into hysteria.

"Is that why you up this early on a Saturday morning?" Grandma turned from tending to the grits on the stove and looked at me, already knowing the answer. "Did you go to sleep at all or did you stay up staring at the ceiling?"

"Yes ma'am, I went to sleep."

"You went right to sleep?" She asked waiting to see if I'd be honest.

"No ma'am."

She shook her head, turning back around to stir the grits. "I sholl hate that boy played that evil joke on you. His Mama should've tore his tail up."

Deacon Willie died. His funeral was at the Juda Christian Baptist Church in Chicago. Mama's church. We had to be there early before the wake started so Mama could cook in the kitchen again. Aaron, one of the teenagers, asked if I wanted to go see the man in the casket. I said okay. I was five years old. He picked me up, took me to the front of the church and placed me inside the casket right on top of the dead man. I stiffened up. I squeezed my eyes shut. I peed. They laughed. He got me out. I stood frozen in place next to the casket, too afraid to look at the dead man whose chest I'd been placed on. He and his friends were still laughing.

I wasn't sure how I made it to the kitchen to tell Mama, except, I couldn't say anything. I stood in front of her frozen, with pee-stained panties that seeped through to my dress. I cried uncontrollably, pointing toward the sanctuary. "What's wrong? What happened?" She and the other women asked. Mama grabbed me, picked me up, stood me on one of the tables, looked me over asking, "How did this happen? Why is your dress wet?"

She pulled the dress off right there in the middle of the kitchen. One of the other ladies got towels, soap and water. I don't remember what happened with the panties. One of the teenagers who laughed answered, "Aaron was just playing with her." They turned in his direction, looking at him, waiting for him to continue. "He asked if she wanted to see the man in the casket and then he put her in there with him." His laughter was broken by a loud gasp. In unison, all the women yelled, "WHAT!" That was the day the spirit of fear introduced itself to me and became an unwanted companion.

Grandma's voice snapped me back to attention. "Did you hear what I said? You can't be listening to them two. I told you ain't nothing to be scared of. The dead can't do nothing to you. Ain't no ghosts running around here or anywhere else for that matter. It's these ones living you need to be worrying about." I shrugged while her back was still turned, eyeing the big orange tiger on the Frosted Flakes box sitting on top of the refrigerator. Close by were the Captain Crunch, Fruit Loops and Apple Jacks, all my favorites. My eyes shifted from one box to the other.

"Can I have some cereal please?"

"No. You gonna eat some of these hot grits, eggs, and sausage I cooked."

I poked my lips out in protest.

"What's wrong with your lips?" Granddaddy said, standing in the doorway of the kitchen. "I see you up early asking about that cereal. You love your cereal."

I hopped from the chair and ran straight into his arms.

"I had to make sure you had your cereal," he chuckled.

"Thank you Granddaddy." I hugged his neck and gave him a kiss on his shiny cheek before taking my seat back at the table. He was fully dressed in a black 3-piece suit and his hat he always cocked to the side.

"Well, Babe, I'm leaving for the meeting now."

"You don't want nothing to eat, preacher?" Grandma asked.

"No. They'll have breakfast there." After a light kiss on her cheek, he was out the door.

"Hurry up and finish your breakfast so you can go upstairs and bathe. Get your clothes packed up. Wake up your sister, too. You all's plane leaving early in the morning."

"Yes ma'am."

I was already on the sixth step when she yelled, "You can't go outside until everything is done."

"Yes ma'am." I said loudly from the top of the stairs. Gina and I were leaving for Chicago at 8am. Auntie already washed my hair and braided it, ready for the hot comb. She would kill me if I got it dirty again. We'd already got the lecture about laying out our Sunday clothes because we were getting back just in time for morning service.

NEW ORLEANS 1975

I opened the bedroom door and walked across the squeaky hardwood floor toward the windows.

"You bet not open them curtains."

I turned around to find Gina still lying down with the covers slightly covering her head. I ignored her and opened the curtains to reveal the identical house next door and light from the sun.

"Grandma said, get up," I whined.

A pillow hit the back of my head.

"I told you not to open the curtains. Now, get out!"

"No! Grandma said get up and make sure our bags are packed. She said we have to leave early in the morning. She said she didn't want us to go outside and play until everything was done. I'm gonna tell you hit me."

"So, I don't care," she scoffed.

I stormed out of the room, headed down the hallway towards the stairs and ran right into Auntie.

"Where you think you going? Didn't Mother tell you to do something?"

How did she know what Grandma said? I thought she was still sleep.

"Yes, but Gina…."

"Girl, stop being a tattle tale."

"But, Auntie, she hit me with a pillow," I whined.

15

"I said go back and finish."

I reluctantly turned around and went back. Gina was up when I went back into the bedroom. I rushed past her, hoping she wouldn't hit me or throw something at my head again.

Stooping down to pull my Charlie Brown and Lucy suitcase from under the bed, I rushed to get back up just in case she had ideas of throwing another pillow at me again. I turned around to look in her direction and instead of her looking at me she was grabbing her things out of her dresser drawers. I hurried to put my Downy smelling clothes and underwear Grandma washed the day before into the suitcase. I placed my sandals neatly on the sides of my suitcase, ribbons, barrettes and earrings in a plastic bag neatly tucked away in the zipper part, just like Mama showed me.

All I wanted to do was to go outside and play. Gina knew and reminded me. "Don't forget, Grandma wants us to lay out our clothes for church to wear on the plane."

"Okay," I responded.

She left me in the bedroom still getting my stuff together. After packing all of my stuff, I made sure I kept my baby doll out so I could play with her later. Grandma was finished cleaning the kitchen and was already in the family room when I came running downstairs.

"Remember what I said about your hair," she said without taking her eyes off the television.

"Yes ma'am," I yelled back while running outside to play.

CHAPTER 4

Got Good Religion

GINA AND I were up early the next morning all ready to head to the airport for our Delta flight back to Chicago. Mama's airline of choice from New Orleans to Chicago and back was always Delta. I was adorned in my Sunday clothes with my hair newly pressed and styled in two long ponytails with perfect curls at the ends. Auntie hot combed my hair the night before, perfectly parted down the middle of my head and placed pink sponge rollers at the end of each ponytail. She'd tied it down with a scarf and sent me to bed warning me not to mess it up.

We made it back to Chicago just in time for Sunday morning service, nice and full from the breakfast the nice flight attendant served us on the plane. Mama and one of her usher friends were standing at the Delta arrival gate waiting as Gina and I came off the plane. After a few minutes of hugs and kisses, Mama was dragging me by the hand through the airport, with Gina lagging behind, towards the baggage claim and into the parking garage.

"We need to hurry up so we can make it before Devotion. I knew we were going to miss Sunday school, but I don't want to miss the Devotion too," Mama said while speed walking.

TORN BIBLE

I didn't understand. Why she was so in a hurry and so excited about Devotion? It was always the same songs and the same prayer we heard Sunday after Sunday.

Faaaatherrrrr iiiiii stre etch my I hand to ooooo thee. No uh thu helllllpppp iiii know. Iiiiiiffff thouuu wiiit draaaw thyyyyy sellllffff froooommmm me, Ohhh whi ther shallll iiii go.

Then the prayer, while people hummed. "Father, Here we are, once mo' and again. Thank You, Lord, for my lying down last night and my early rising this morning. Thank You that my bed was not my cooling board. Please suh, look and have mercy."

It didn't matter which deacon prayed or which mother sang, they said the same thing. I didn't know what a cooling board was. Who was suh? What was he supposed to be looking at and what did having mercy mean? I didn't ask because I didn't want to get popped in my mouth for being disrespectful.

I sat on the pew right in front of the door playing with my Baby Alive, where Mama could keep a watchful eye from her post on the Usher Board. The pastor preached about your flight not being in winter. He read from the gospel of Matthew. He quickly went from a low tone to a high boom while the musician played accompanying music on the organ. After thirty minutes he calmed down, while a lady adorned in a white dress and a nurses hat, put a black cape around his shoulders and used a white handkerchief to wipe his face.

The women stopped screaming, "Go head, yes Lord and thank ya Jesus." They stood with hands raised. The pastor slowly talked, making sure everyone heard every word, about Jesus dying on the cross for our sins and getting saved from hell.

He then announced, "Will there be one to come by Christian

experience or by letter." I didn't know what all that meant, but I decided to take that long walk down the center aisle to be saved from hell. Mama told me I was christened as a baby, but getting "saved" was always my choice once I reached an age of reasoning.

The huge cross in the ceiling seemed brighter than usual. The usher that was in charge of the light made sure to turn it on when the pastor, adorned with whatever priestly robe he chose to wear on any given Sunday, made his entrance into service. As soon as he made it to the center of the aisle, the cross lit up a bold red color. When I made it to the front and sat in one of the two chairs the deacon placed out front, the pastor asked, "Do you believed that Jesus died for your sins on the cross, was buried in a tomb and rose again on the third day?" I confidently said yes.

I'd heard about Jesus many times. Granddaddy always talked about Him. When he prayed, he always ended with "in Jesus' name." I believed my Granddaddy when he talked about Jesus dying and I believed the pastor too. I confessed like the pastor said to do and was confirmed and saved from eternal damnation. My pastor announced, "Upon the confession of your faith and obedience to the great head of the church, you are saved." I felt relieved. I wasn't going to hell anymore.

The next Sunday I was baptized. The deacons moved all of the chairs where the mother's board sat. They lifted the floor to expose the pool that was underneath. My pastor and another minister stood side by side in black robes while the congregation sang *Take me to the Water*."

The mothers dressed us in white gowns and white swimming caps. We stood in a long line and waited for our turn. I tried to be brave, but the pastor's black robe looked scary. One by one we each had to stand in the middle of the pastor and the associate minister with our hands across our chest while the pastor said, "In obedience to Jesus Christ, the great head of the church. I baptize you in the name of the Father, in the name of the Son, in the name of the Holy Ghost, Amen." He put his big hand over my mouth and nose and scooped me down in the water.

Mama made sure, when we were in Chicago, Gina and I were busy in church. It was a routine of Sunday school, all day church services, chicken and fish dinners, midweek services and choir rehearsals. I was the youngest member of the junior choir and the combined choir. We sang all of the latest gospel hits. We visited other churches and went to endless musicals and special memorial midnight concerts. All of the musical activities, countless road trips and trying out different restaurants on Friday nights made church social. I never once thought church was about faith or growth. It was just social and fun with a little Jesus mixed in.

The pastor was larger than life. He was a big man with a big voice that boomed throughout the church. He hooped or hacked when he preached and every time he did, the people were on their feet with loud voices of, "Amen Reverend and yeah Lord" coming from all corners of the building. I thought he sounded like he was having a hard time breathing, but no one else seemed to mind. He stood on the pews. He walked the isles. He sang *Precious Lord Take My Hand* and *I Stood on the Banks of the Jordan to See the Ships Go By*. Before he could get the first note out, women would start screaming and hollering. Some women fell out on the floor.

I could never understand all the fuss. I found safe corners to stand in, far away from swinging arms, flying wigs and hats. I watched people run around the church, watched women lose slips, and saw dentures falling out a time or two. All of this on account of people "catching the Holy Ghost." I never aspired to "catch the Holy Ghost," because "it" made people act crazy and dangerous.

GOT GOOD RELIGION

I'd learned my lesson after one lady Mama sat me next to "got happy" and started swinging her arms. She hit me in the face. I hit her back. She told Mama I hit her after service. Mama interrogated me.

"Why did you do that? Why did you hit that lady?"

"She hit me first," I protested. "She knew I was sitting there and she hit me."

"But she was shouting. She didn't mean to hit you," Mama retorted.

I said, "So. I still think she did know."

Mama popped me in the mouth. From that day on, I stayed away from swinging arms.

Every Sunday I asked Mama the same questions. "Why are they singing about looking at ships going by and where are the ships going? What are the banks of Jordan? Is it the same Jordan in the Bible? Why are Mary weeping and Martha moaning? What does Pharaoh's army drowning in the Red Sea have to do with Mary weeping and Martha moaning? Isn't one story in the Old Testament and another one in the New Testament?"

Mama would entertain my questions and answer to the best of her ability. Some answers she didn't have and she said as much.

I remembered Granddaddy preaching about Lazarus and his sisters. Lazarus died when Jesus didn't come on time to heal him. He showed me his Bible when I would see him studying. In my seven year old brain, I concluded that maybe that's why Mary was weeping and Martha was moaning. They were sad. They were angry at Jesus for showing up after their brother was already dead. Pharaoh and his army was a whole other story closer to the front of the Bible. Although

TORN BIBLE

I tried to understand, I couldn't make out what one had to do with the other.

The pastor always preached about God being a loving God, powerful, sitting high and looking low. I didn't understand the sitting high and looking low part. All the other attributes seemed easy to believe. God sent His Son to die for all who believe. That's love. God just seemed too big for a child like me to reach, but my pastor seemed really close to Him. I thought he knew God better than anyone, except my Granddaddy, Grandma and Mama. I heard the grown folk say the pastor was God's mouthpiece. Whatever he spoke, it was like God speaking through him. I imagined an old man with a long gray beard sitting high on a throne and looking down as low as can be to see all of the little people He created.

CHAPTER 5

Don't Tell

MAMA SENT ME to Vacation Bible School at the church one summer. It was 1978. I was ten years old. Instead of learning Bible stories, I learned how to grind. I learned how to lie on my back and let a man climb on top. I learned about sex. 1978, the year my body grew up. 1978, the year I lost my voice, the year I disappeared. 1978, the year I was repeatedly molested by the church janitor. It went on undetected. I went undetected. The janitor asked me if I wanted to help him clean the pastor's office. It was free time and most of the kids went outside to play while the adults sat around talking.

I wasn't the kid who rushed outside to play in Chicago. I didn't have many friends to play jump rope and hopscotch with. The grown folk in charge of Bible school didn't insist on me going out to play with the other kids. They dismissed for lunch and recess and didn't seem to mind what the kids wanted to do. They didn't bother to look for me on days when I'd disappear for more than an hour or two. The grown folk who gave more free time than Bible story time didn't know what was happening right under their noses.

I loved my pastor and I thought it would be fun to help keep his office clean. More fun than playing Tag or It with the kids I didn't have anything in common with. I reached for the rag and the lemon Pledge sitting conveniently on a folding table next to a chair. Clearing his desk, the smell of lemon nearly choked me as I wiped and scrubbed. The janitor vacuumed the carpet and offered me candy as payment for helping him that first day. The next day the janitor asked if I was still going to help him. I said, "You want me to dust again?"

He said, "You did such a good job yesterday. You can help wipe down the sofa." It was a dark brown leather sofa that sat on one side of the office with two brown high back chairs on the other side.

I happily wiped down the sofa and after the office was filled with the smell of lemon, I announced that I was finished with my dusting job. Instead of giving me candy, he reached out, took me by my hand and pulled me close to him.

He hugged me and whispered in my ear, "Thanks."

His hands slowly moved from around my shoulders toward my back and down to my butt. I tried pushing away, but he tightened his grip. I could feel his breath on my neck.

I squirmed and mumbled, "No. Stop it. I'm telling. No. No. No."

"Tell who? Who are you going to tell? No one's going to believe you. Besides, there's nothing to tell. We're not doing anything wrong. It's just a game. Just think how proud pastor will be, knowing you helped keep his office clean." All the while he's talking, he's feeling and touching. He said, "It's our secret and our special relationship." I tried pushing him again, but he just got angrier. His skin looked darker, if that was even possible. His eyes looked dark red. I was so terrified to look at him. I shut my eyes tight, still squirming to break free.

"Look, I'll make sure Pastor knows how much you helped with his office. Okay? He'll be proud of you. So, just stop acting like that. I already told you, we're not doing anything wrong." It didn't seem right. It wasn't right. But, he'd convinced me that no one would believe me, especially the pastor. This continued throughout the duration of Vacation Bible School. I tried to act like nothing was happening and continued to participate in the daily activities. I tried to sing the songs and memorize the Bible stories. But, day after day, it was the same. He touched, kissed, felt and made me lay down on the couch in pastor's office while he made weird movements on top. He said the game was called grinding. He said I needed to promise not to tell anyone about our game.

My pastor saw me coming out of his office one day during the last week of Vacation Bible School. He'd normally be in and out taking care of church business or fixing on the church's buses and van. I ran to him just knowing I was being rescued. I ran to him, ready to tell everything the janitor said was secret. I was going to tell him about the game the janitor was making me play, he would make him stop and throw him out the church. Frantically, I said the janitor's name and proceeded to try and tell what happened.

"Reb!" I couldn't say reverend too good. "I gotta tell you something."

He looked as if I was interrupting wherever he was headed.

"Allen said I could help with cleaning your office and he said you'd be proud, and"

His eyes shifted from me to the janitor who was coming out of the office.

"What were you doing in my office with him?" He asked in an accusatory tone.

Clearly he didn't hear me say I was helping to clean the office. Instead of repeating that part, I answered, trying to speed talk.

TORN BIBLE

"Allen is doing these things and he's touching me all the time. He said it was a game, and he said... and I don't know....."

He interrupted me and said, "You're growing up and developing fast for your age. He took a quick glance at my size B cup breasts.

"You can't be around here acting fast. You need stay away from... him."

He quickly brushed past me as if I was a little pest he wanted to get away from. His face was void of emotion. Nothing was between us except cool air that didn't come from the fan blowing from the corner of the room. It was my fault. He looked at my size B cup breasts. My breasts were too big for a ten year old. I was being fast. That's what he said. That's how he saw me. That's how God saw me, right? He was God's mouthpiece, right? He was God's representative, right? That's what the grown folk said. I turned to see him walk into his office without so much as a word or a look back at me.

Did he think I told a story? Mama said I couldn't use the word, lie. Did he believe me, but didn't care? I didn't know what to do or what to think. I couldn't tell Mama. If he, my own pastor didn't do anything or didn't believe me, she wouldn't either. Mama's a faithful member of the church. We were always there. She held auxiliary leadership positions, was a regular cook in the kitchen, she had lots of friends, and on and on. There was no way she'd believe me. That's what I thought. That's what I said to myself.

I couldn't say for certain if the pastor said or did anything to the janitor or not. I just knew he was still at church working in ministry on Sundays, and cleaning and fixing things Monday through Saturday. All I knew was at ten years old, I had to protect myself. I spent years trying to, as the pastor said, stay away from the janitor. I was afraid to look in his direction during services, during Bible classes and during church outings. I was afraid to go to the restroom alone and afraid to go hang up my coat in the closet alone. I was afraid of being alone at church so the janitor wouldn't attack me again. I was just afraid all of time.

CHAPTER **6**

Secrets and Chaos

1968 WAS THE year of civil unrest and fights for rights for black folks. 1968 was the year of the assassinations of Dr. Martin Luther King Jr. and Robert F. Kennedy. 1968 was the year of soul music hits. It was April 19th, three weeks after Dr. Martin Luther King Jr's murder. April 4th 1968 was the day hope died. The black ghettos of America burned out of anger, frustration and lost purpose. Mama was sick with preeclampsia and high blood pressure and was placed on bed rest.

No doubt pressure from the nation's chaos as well as her own inner turmoil caused her to go into labor early. I was premature, eight months. Mama said I wasn't breathing when I was born. I was sick and had to be left at the hospital after doctors released her. She said I cried a lot when I came home. I cried and cried. She said I was a friendly child, but super sensitive and serious. I lacked humor. She said I had strong feelings, felt things deeply, and picked up on other peoples' emotions. I grew up and still cried.

I wanted Gina to know what it was like to feel alone. I wanted her to know what it felt like to be talked about, gossiped about, and whispered about. I wanted her to share my life and my feelings. That way, she would know what it was like to be me. I could have her to talk to. She and I could share stories of Sunday shenanigans, how we felt about the other family that didn't want us in their lives. But it was just me, me with no one to know how I felt. There was no one to empathize. There was no one to know what it was like to be me.

I wanted her dad. Her dad was cool, quiet, and friendly. He treated me like I mattered. He talked to me and gave me money to buy Boston Baked Beans, Jolly Ranchers and Lemon Heads from the candy store. Her dad loved her. Her dad loved me too. Her dad didn't deny her. I really wanted her dad. She had her own friends and interesting activities. She had her own life that was vastly different than mine. She didn't have much in common with me because she was much older.

I was always tip toeing at church. It was a medium size church. Bigger than a store front, but much smaller than a mega church. It was small enough to know everybody and everything about everybody. I stumbled into private conversations between women on the Mothers' Board and women on the Usher Board. I, unintentionally, crept into the end of words and sentences at holiday dinners. "She sholl do look just like him."

"Girl, you know that's Deacon Jackson's daughter?"

"Who? Sharon?"

"Yeah. Can't you tell? I can't believe you didn't know?"

"I heard something about it, but I didn't want to go asking around."

"What? Everybody knows."

"Yeah, you know he was still married when he started seeing her mother, and not too far after that child was born, his wife fell dead."

TORN BIBLE

"You kidding. I didn't know all of that."

"Yeah, it was sudden, I think."

I wasn't eavesdropping. I was just walking around, walking through the church between services. I was walking into the kitchen for chicken wings and fries or into the ladies restroom to….. There weren't many places to go while people waited for the next service to start. There weren't many places to go to not over hear all the gossip, all the talk about stuff, and all the talk about me. Everybody knew. Maybe they found out about the janitor. Of course everyone knew I was the product of an affair. They knew who my daddy was. They knew who his children were because they were members of the church too.

I never knew the details of his membership status. I just knew he was a deacon. He sat on the Deacon Board whenever he came to the church. He never said much to me when he was at church. His children, who were all adults, didn't say much of anything at all. Whenever he came for a visit, he'd come as far as the living room near the front door. He never sat down to stay a while. He'd pat me on the head like I was a pet instead of a child, his child. His conversations were limited to my hair, my looks, what I wanted to be when I grew up and here's ten dollars. That exchange took all of ten minutes, tops.

Sometimes he'd call and say he was on his way to see me. I'd look out the window waiting for him to show up, but more times than not, he didn't show up. The older I grew, the less I believed him or looked for him. As I understood it, Mama found out he lied about his marital status. He was still married when she started seeing him and became pregnant. She made the right decision to stop seeing him, but decided to have and raise me on her own. She stayed at the Juda Christian church. I didn't understand why she liked it there so much. I didn't understand why she stayed. That church for me was the church of unending rejection. It was the church of elephants in the room, me being one of them. It was the church where I saw people I looked like, but they wanted nothing to do with me.

My life was as divided as night and day. One part of my life was in New Orleans where I was happy and carefree. I played jump rope, hopscotch, jacks, and hide and seek. I played with cousins and bounced around between my Grandparents', Aunts' and Uncles' homes. New Orleans is where we took street cars to Canal St. and the French Quarter during the day. Grandma said be home before dark because that was no place for kids at night. New Orleans' lower ninth ward was where I stayed days at a time with one of my aunts and cousins.

My cousins and I looked forward to going to Lake Pontchartrain Amusement Park. We daydreamed about the houses we'd buy in the Garden District or other upper class areas while we made mud pies outside Auntie Sally's lower ninth ward project apartment. The projects were where we spied on couples kissing and groping each other in the hallways.

In New Orleans I didn't have to think about the janitor. In New Orleans I had a real family. Nobody whispered about me. Nobody asked questions about who my daddy was and who I looked like. I was free to be a kid and free to be me.

The other part of my life was foggy and gray. It was Chicago. Chicago was the big city with famous mobsters, corrupt politicians, and tall buildings like the Sears Tower, John Hancock Building and Water Tower Place. Chicago was the place Frank Sinatra sang about. Chicago was the place I was fearful. I was scared to go to sleep. It was the place I had nightmares. When I closed my eyes, I saw the dead man. I saw the janitor and his charcoal ashy skin. I smelled his scent. I still tasted his kisses with his tongue. It was the place I always felt sick.

TORN BIBLE

Chicago was where I slept during the day when I should've been playing outside. I stayed in my room and read books. I escaped to Little House on the Prairie and The Walton's. I visualized myself being one of the March sisters in Little Women. I took Margaret's place in her letters to God in Dear God, It's Me, Margaret. I watched the Brady Bunch and Speed Racer with Kenny who lived up the street.

Kenny was my best friend. We were kindred spirits. We both had complicated lives at ten and eleven years old. He lived with his grandma and granddaddy too. I wrote to him whenever I wasn't in Chicago. His parental situation was just as confusing as mine. I spent hours of days down at his house. I sought refuge in his home over Checkers and play fights. We shared sadness like other kids our age shared imaginary stories.

We didn't want to only exist because of the choices our parents made. We didn't want to be the topic of discussions over dinner tables. Our scandal filled lives forced us to grow up quicker than we wanted and have conversations no child should have and emotions that should be reserved for adulthood. And yet, we still had secrets we chose not to tell each other. But, in moments of awkward silence, we knew.

We sat together on the love seat in his grandparent's house when his mom died. The two of us watched as people came and went. We watched as people whispered to each other. We knew something was wrong. There was something about the whispers, something other than his mom's death. One of them whispered suicide to the other. Neither one of us said anything. We didn't know what that word meant and we didn't ask questions. I sat at home with him when his family thought it best not to take him to the funeral. We watched television. When he wanted to talk, I listened. He asked why he couldn't go see his mom. Why he couldn't say goodbye. He asked why they wouldn't let him go. I didn't know why. I didn't have answers. But, I understood sadness. He was my friend, so I just listened.

So, now when we went to church, I disappeared. Even though I was visible to other people, I wasn't there. I sat alone in corners with my eyes roaming around trying to keep an eye out for the janitor. I sang in the choir. I went to choir rehearsal. I watched and listened to people I shared DNA with work in ministry. I learned songs about Jesus loving little children.

I didn't believe it anymore. I didn't feel like a precious little girl anymore. I slept. I looked forward to going back to New Orleans and leaving Chicago permanently. Grandma was sickly though. I watched her take pills from different pill bottles she had on her table. She had arthritis really bad in her hands and I'd help her with her medicine. I didn't care about that. I was going back. I was going back, until Grandma died. There was no need to go back after she died. It wasn't the same without her.

Mama was extremely attentive and went out of her way to make my life a little easier. She knew it was hard. I tried to make the best of it. I tried to be okay. I tried to be happy but I was sad. Mama was starting to ask questions more often.

"Sharon, are you okay? What's wrong, honey? Why don't you come out of that room and look at television with me and Gina?"

"Yes ma'am. I'm okay. I'm just reading."

Getting lost in books and being alone in my room felt safe. I could escape into another world because my own world was scary. My reality was uncomfortable and painful. I didn't have the words to tell her what I was feeling because I didn't know what I was feeling.

Mama came home from work one day and announced she'd scheduled an appointment for me to see a doctor. I assumed it was with my regular pediatrician, Dr. Keith. It was a new doctor, a lady with a short afro and ashy lips, who sat in a chair behind a desk and asked annoying questions I couldn't answer.

"Why do you like sitting off in a corner by yourself? Your mom tells me you seem unhappy. Is that true?"
I shrugged my shoulders, not knowing how to answer her.

"Would you like to tell me anything, anything at all?"

What was I supposed to say to her? She was really making me mad. I slumped down in the chair and answered, "No!" I'd hoped she'd stop talking.

A few years passed with constant bus trips from the west side to the north side of Chicago to see the doctor therapist. I didn't like her, but Mama thought, by some miracle, she would get through to me. She eventually stopped taking me to see her. She figured it wasn't helping very much anyway. I'd hear her praying a lot. She was praying for me. She bought me my own Bible. She bought new baby dolls and tea sets. She bought more interesting African American books and a new set of encyclopedias.

I spent each waking moment reading about Black History, autobiographies, literature and art. I played house or beauty shop by myself. She tried her best to make sure I had what I needed and some of the things I wanted. She took me on weekly bus trips to Michigan Ave. We'd visit Water Tower Place or take long walks down Michigan Avenue to visit different shops. By age thirteen, I had a passport. We took trips every year throughout the Midwest, throughout the South, and all the way to the Bahamas. She did everything she could to help me, except one thing, church. I wanted her to leave church. I wanted her to leave that church. I could never ask her to leave or ask why she stayed.

She taught me Bible scriptures. It was her way of trying to teach me coping skills. She helped me memorize Psalm 23 and John 3:16. She said whenever I felt lonely or sad, say these scriptures. The Lord is my Shepherd and I shall not want. For God so loved the World that He gave His only begotten Son. I wasn't feeling shepherded or loved, but she wasn't deterred. She and I got down on our knees to say the Lord's Prayer every day. At bed time it was, "Now I lay me down to sleep, I pray the Lord my soul to keep. If I should die before I wake, I pray the Lord my soul to take." By the time I turned thirteen, not waking up seemed more appealing than waking up.

CHAPTER 7

Deacon Jackson

HIS NAME IS Deacon Jackson. I never called him dad again. The man everyone said I looked like and walked like was Deacon Jackson. The man I was told couldn't deny me had denied me. I'd called his house to talk with him. A woman, I assumed was his new wife, answered.

"Hi. May I speak with Deacon Jackson?"

After a sigh and a dry, "hold on," I could hear her telling him something I couldn't make out and then he was on the phone.

"Hello?"

"Hi Dad. It's me, Sharon."

"Oh. Uh… Hi. Listen, you can't call here anymore. It's just not a good idea for you to call here."

And with that, he hung up. I held the receiver in my hand, so my reflex could catch up with what had just happened.

It felt like my heart stopped for a second. Once his words registered,

I slammed the phone down and ran into my bedroom, lay across the bed and cried my eyes out. Mama ran into the room after me.

"What's wrong? Why are you crying? I thought you were on the phone with your dad," she interrogated. Between sobs, I told her.

"He said I can't call his house anymore. He said it wasn't a good idea. Why would he say that to me?"

She immediately started apologizing to me for what he said. I looked over at her and saw her eyes glossed over.

"Baby, I'm so sorry this happened."

After consoling me a little while longer, she was on the phone talking with one of his sisters, the one aunt who never denied me. She was the aunt who called me Peewee. Mama was telling her what happened. I'm not sure what their resolution was, but I knew what my resolution was.

This rejection wasn't the first time he'd said I wasn't his daughter or that he didn't want me. I was too young or still in Mama's womb to know about all the drama that unfolded. I learned some it from the gossiping women at church. I'd learned a whole lot more many years later from people who I never knew were looking out for me and protecting me. I learned some of it from him. Mama told me more when she felt I was old enough.

She said a few of his children used to care about me as a baby, but she didn't really know what happened to make them stop caring. She said she had an idea, but wasn't sure. She didn't want to speculate. None of that mattered to me because they didn't care to know me when it mattered, and just like Deacon Jackson, they'd rejected me too.

TORN BIBLE

The year before Deacon Jackson told me not to call his house anymore I'd gotten the number of one of his daughters and called her. I was eleven years old.

"Hello," she answered.

"Hi. How are you?" I asked.

"Who is this?"

"This is Sharon," I said in my carefree cheerful voice.

"How did you get this number?" She snapped.

I said, "Mama had it."

"Well, don't call me again." She hung up.

I told Mama what she said to me.

She said, "Don't call her anymore."

I didn't call her ever again, not even years later, when she wanted me to.

Deacon Jackson eventually came back around to whatever apartment we were living in at the time. Mama would open the door and let him into the living room.

"Sharon."

She'd call me to come to the living room. I'd slowly stroll in and quickly sit down on the ugly green paisley couch that showed up at every apartment we moved into.

"Hi, Share," he'd say. He couldn't say Sharon.

"Hi, Deacon Jackson," I'd answer.

"Deacon Jackson? You call me Deacon Jackson now?"

"Yes," I sighed.

"It's yes sir to you. I'm still your dad."

I was a deer caught in headlights, confused. Yes sir? dad? Was I really supposed to play this is-he-or-is-he-ain't-my-daddy game? I knew I couldn't say what I was thinking out loud, but I was going through serious turmoil. All I could muster up was "Okay."

He never mentioned the phone incident again, but I never forgot. No matter what he said or thought, I was never calling him dad ever again nor did I give him the yes sir, no sir he wanted.

He'd continue with his usual.

"You look just like…

Your hair is so long and pretty…

What do you want to be when you grow up?"

I endured never ending tugs of my hair, weird face inspections, awkward hugs and a reach 'n his pocket to give me ten dollars until the next time he came for a drive through. That was it. The relationship, if that's what you want to call it, was limited to the living room of our apartment until I was eighteen.

I still had to see them, all of them at church all the time. It didn't change the fact I had to watch him sit with the other deacons whenever he showed up there. It was confusing to hear him sing a Doctor Watts or pray a prayer. It didn't help that I had to listen to them or watch them work in ministry. One of the few times they paid attention to me was when they wanted to record an album and wanted me to sing soprano.

Mama was the only one excited about it. I had no interest in singing with them. They didn't talk to me. We didn't have a relationship. Why would I want to sing with them? Mama convinced me it would be the right thing to do. I endured awkward rehearsals and studio sessions. After the recordings were over, it was back to the rejection. I felt like a yoyo. They pulled me in to sing and pushed me out when I finished recording. I was pulled in briefly when my friend was alive and back out when he died.

Part 2
Looking For Jesus - Finding Religion

1982-2009

CHAPTER 8

Private Schools

MAMA SENT ME to private (Catholic) schools. Grade school uniforms consisted of scotch tape skirts, little gold ties that wrapped around white Peter Pan collar blouses. Even in middle school, I was extremely serious to be a little girl. Being around kids my own age in school didn't change the fact I had to grow up faster than normal. I felt like I was older. I had trouble laughing at dumb jokes most kids thought was funny. I had trouble making friends with girls my age because I thought they were silly. I thought they cared about dumb stuff that made no sense to me. I had better conversations with the nuns and the other teachers.

High school was surprisingly much better. I still had to wear uniforms of scotch tape skirts, white blouses and green or blue sweaters in the winter. Mama said public school wasn't for me. She said I was too reserved-too shy-too sensitive. She said I wouldn't fit in with the ghetto, loud talking kids who liked to fight and lived in the neighborhood. After graduating from St. Mary of Angels, I had a choice between Notre Dame and Madonna all girls' high schools. I chose Madonna because it felt more quaint and friendly. Madonna was a relatively small school compared to most high schools and had a more diverse student body.

My days started at six o'clock in the morning and ended at six o'clock in the evening, sometimes later. I took two buses to the northwest side of Chicago and back every day. On the bus is where I realized Mama was right about fitting in with the other kids. The kids from several public high schools took the same Austin or Central Ave bus routes I took to school. Some of them were loud and rude to other passengers, cussed out the bus driver for sport and picked fights. They liked sitting in the back of the bus, so I made sure to sit in the front of the bus. I sat on the side seats near the bus driver with a book to read and my Walkman to listen to music. I kept my head phones on my ears and pretended not to hear them talking about me and the other kids who had on Catholic school uniforms.

Every day I busied myself with extracurricular activities that took up time. Time I didn't have to spend thinking about my life. I sang in chorus. I relished early morning and after school rehearsals. I participated in school plays. I supported friends who were athletes. I went to all of the basketball, softball games and track meets. I was the designated wall flower at school dances, only dancing occasionally when a song I really liked came on. I hung out at diners with friends, most of whom looked different than me.

I attended Mass once a month and during some school days. I already knew the Lord's Prayer. I learned The Hail Mary and The Rosary prayers. I knew when to stand, when to kneel and when to sit in mass. The nuns, adorned in their habits, black or brown uniform dresses and loafer shoes, always kept a stern eye on all the girls with a ruler handy to make sure we were on our best behavior.

The Catholic Bible was a mandatory book for school. Each student was required to take a religion class all four years of school. The Catholic Bible consists of 73 books, which included the Apocrypha, instead of the 66 books in the Protestant Bible. Mary was to be revered, honored and prayed to. I also had to know which saint to pray to for whatever situation I found myself in. It wasn't like the King James Bible I knew about. In the King James Bible, Mary was the mother of Jesus. She was someone to be respected, but not worshipped.

Their Bible said Jesus was the son of God, He was crucified, died and was resurrected. But, in the Catholic Bible, Mary was assumed or taken up to heaven. They believe you can pray to Mary too. I found myself in a bit of a conflict because I didn't believe a lot of what was in their bible. It was way too much for me to remember. I just couldn't keep all of the saints and their different prayers straight.

I asked Mama about it and showed her the Bible I had to read for religion class. She said, "Just read it enough to pass tests and the class. Write what they want you to write, say what they want you to say, but you don't have to believe any of it."

That solution worked well. I did what she said and got A's throughout all four years. Catholicism for me was a confusing and complicated religion. I had a hard time comprehending most of it. After graduating from high school, I never went to another mass.

I ended up at a junior college the following January after Grandma died. I hadn't figured out what I wanted to do after my plans of going back to Louisiana were shattered. School became an afterthought. It was something to do every morning before going to work in the evenings. I didn't have a field of study narrowed down, so a less expensive option of junior college was a better decision. It soon became a welcomed distraction. I quickly fell in love with academia. It didn't hurt that I was already nerdy and thought hanging out in the library and at bookstores was exciting.

I continued my academic education at DePaul University. Being the bookworm that I am, I majored in English Literature. I absolutely loved my academic career and vowed to always be a life student. I participated in interesting writing groups, book clubs, met wonderful people, developed great relationships with professors and made at least one lifelong friend.

I was also expanding my church experiences. At nineteen, with the help of a few friends," I started visiting Sunday night musicals and broadcasts at a local Church Of God In Christ. I didn't know anything about the religion. It was drastically different than the Baptist traditions I was used to. I loved the pastor. He was a wonderful teacher and had a way of making the Bible come alive for me. Most people I knew went for the choir and the music, but what impacted me was the teaching. It was different from what I'd heard before. It wasn't a lot of whooping and hollering. I understood every word he was saying from beginning to end.

I faithfully attended Sunday school and listened to the Sunday School Commentary every Saturday night on the radio. I soon became fascinated with the Bible. I began trying to read more and more on my own. But, I didn't know how to ask or pray for revelation or how to interpret scripture properly. I just considered the Bible interesting reading loaded with ancient history, fascinating poetry and intriguing parables and life lessons. I began visiting this church more and more. Soon, people at my church started asking me why I was going to "that" church. I didn't have any answers. It was hard to put into words what I was feeling when I went there so, I just said, "It's different."

All I knew was I wanted to leave. I'd always wanted to leave. I wanted to start over. I didn't know who I was. I wanted and needed love, but felt more like I was hated instead. I wanted to believe and trust in the God who I heard about every week. But, I didn't trust Him. I figured I needed to do something else and then maybe I'd be good enough for God/Jesus to want and love me. I could learn to trust Him.

CHAPTER 9

Rape and Suicide Attempts

I MET THIS really nice minister at a church Mama's church fellowshipped with. He was dark and handsome with an impeccable taste in clothes. He was fun to be with and well versed in the Bible. Minister James was the perfect gentlemen. He was very respectful and Mama loved him. I never had many boyfriends and the few I did have weren't shy about what they really wanted from me. They didn't last long.

Minister James was different. He held doors for me. He prayed over meals. He prayed over offerings at his church. He read the scriptures at his church. He shared his sermon ideas with me. He studied scripture with me. He prayed all the time. When we took walks, he always made sure I walked on the inside. He'd say, "Men should always walk on the outside for protection." For the first time in my life, I felt like a princess.

We dated for months and not one time did he try anything. We had long talks and great Bible discussions. We talked about literature. We talked about the latest movies. We talked. He knew much more than I did. He was twenty-two and I was nineteen. I picked his brain on a lot of things that interested me. I felt perfectly safe with him. I didn't think anything of it when he came over to visit one day when

RAPE AND SUICIDE ATTEMPTS

I was home alone. It wasn't the first time, so I didn't think anything of it.

He asked for a hug, which I gave. But, as I tried to let go, he held on tighter. The hug quickly escalated to me trying to fight him off. He became angry, grabbing me and calling me horrible names. With his hands over my mouth, he dragged me into my bedroom. Taking his hand off my mouth, he pushed me so hard onto the bed that I hit my head on the corner of the headboard. He slammed the door shut behind him and I began to scream as loud as I could, hoping our upstairs neighbor heard me. I kicked and tried screaming louder, but she didn't hear me and she never came to my rescue. When it was all said and done, I'd been raped, called bitch, spoiled brat, and hoe. He berated me, looked at me with disgust and said everything that happened was my fault.

Just as quickly as he'd attacked me, he started praying. He prayed! He said. "Lord, I pray that you forgive us for what we did. I ask you, Lord, to forgive me for yielding to temptation and forgive Sharon for tempting me."

I stared in disbelief. I didn't know who this person was. It was like two different people. He was a perfect gentleman who'd turned into a monster. He was still praying. "I know You know how women can be, so, Lord, I ask for Your mercy, in Jesus Name, Amen."

I was in shock, this time, staring down at the pool of blood I was sitting in. I didn't know what to do or what to say. I was in so much pain and was so devastated. I couldn't look up. Something in me died again. Without so much as a glance at me, or a word, he put his clothes on and left. I never heard from him again.

I don't remember how long I stayed in that bed, that bed that I couldn't bear to sleep in anymore. I threw the sheets away. I put them into a plastic garbage bag, took them to the alley and put them in a neighbor's garbage dumpster. I was ashamed. I didn't want Mama, Gina or the upstairs neighbor to know. I went into the bathroom. I took a shower. I put on underwear and two sanitary napkins. I took pain medicine, lots of pain medicine. I wanted to sleep and never wake up again. I didn't tell anyone. I rehearsed the prayer he prayed over and over again and wondered if God really listened to him. Did God really forgive him? Did God really blame me? It was my fault again? I did something to cause this again?

The words my pastor said when I was ten came flooding back to my mind. "Don't be fast." That's it. I was fast. No one will believe me. Remember what happened with the janitor? Your pastor didn't do anything when you told him. He probably didn't believe you anyway. You can't tell anyone this time. No one will ever protect you. Just forget it ever happened.

I woke up angry, angry that I woke up. I didn't take enough pain killers. I had severe stomach pains in the days that followed. I wore feminine products longer than should have been necessary. In the months that followed, Mama took me to see my gynecologist because I'd gotten weak and would often pass out. I never told her about the rape. I still hadn't told anyone. I stuffed it way down hoping never to remember it again. The doctor said I needed iron. It was determined that I was severely anemic.

A little over a month later, I was at the doctor again. I was alone. I bled more than I should have and that scared me. The nurse pulled me aside and told me I may have had a miscarriage. I was stoic. She looked for a reaction. She couldn't believe my lack of interest in what she was saying. "You didn't have a full exam the last time you were here?" I didn't remember yesterday. How could I remember the last time I was there? She looked at me with as much compassion as she could muster and assured me that I didn't have to tell my mother.

I didn't tell her. I didn't tell anyone. The doctor at the clinic did a DNC and I went on to stuff my pain deep down into my subconscious. I told myself the rape didn't happen. I said it until I believed it, until I thought it was gone from my memory. I just wanted to forget everything. I wanted to just sleep and sleep and sleep until the last nineteen years of my life were gone. I took as many pills in the medicine cabinet as I could find. I took sleeping pills and pain medicine. I drank lots of water, ignored the stomach pain and nausea, and went to sleep. It was during the day.

It wasn't unusual for me to sleep for hours. I slept all the time. I slept because I didn't want to think. I slept when I didn't want to feel. I slept and slept and slept. I slept because I didn't want to wake up. I woke up later the next day and was angry about it again. It didn't work and I blamed God. I wanted the pain to permanently go away, but I woke up. I woke up to live another day of pain. I tried using a razor blade and a knife to cut my wrist. I bled a lot, but not enough. I cut deep, but not deep enough. I missed my veins. I wrapped my wrists with bandages and wore long sleeves. It was September in Chicago. The chill in the air meant no one would question me. I clearly didn't know what I was doing. I had to come up with another way to die.

The years that followed were filled with more turmoil and more sadness. I started eating less and less. I was down to 100 pounds. Mama worried about the shifts in my mood and weight. This time, after taking me to another doctor she learned I had an eating disorder, anorexia. The doctors and nurses gave her pamphlets and referrals for more therapists. She took it upon herself to make sure I got healthy again. She forced me to sit with her at the table and eat. She watched me like a hawk. Every day for months, I sat at a table for every meal while she coached me to eat. I ate one small bite after another until I'd eaten a full meal. She did this every day until she got me to eat regularly. She wanted to take me back to the doctor, but opted against it. Her prayers were answered and I eventually started getting better.

TORN BIBLE

I took on more and more hours at work. I occupied my time in book stores and libraries when I wasn't working. I was doing any and everything to flood my mind of unwanted thoughts. I visited more churches not because I really wanted to, but because church was all I knew. One church was far advanced in tongue talking and spiritual gifts, which I knew nothing about. So by default and less confusion, I finally settled on the local Church Of God In Christ.

I struggled at the Church Of God In Christ, trying to learn about their way of doing things. I learned their song and sang along at services and annual convocations. I wasn't sure if I was really part of it because Mama, Grandma and Granddaddy raised me in the Baptist church. So, no, I wasn't "born in it." I memorized the scripture, 1 Thessalonians 2:14. I pressed on, faithfully, going to Sunday school, Bible class, studying the Bible and trying to learn how to live a holy life, hoping Jesus would accept me. I listened as it was explained this was the way to Him.

The church mothers and some of the women told me I had to take off my makeup, my short sleeves, my jewelry, my open toed shoes and change the way I wore my hair to be holy, like God. They told me I had to change my appearance to not become a stumbling block to anyone, especially the men of God. I had to wear nylons you couldn't see through. They said I had to be baptized again, tarry and speak in tongues in order to get the Holy Ghost. The Church Of God In Christ didn't take communion every first Sunday like the Baptist church. When I inquired, I was told it didn't have to be every first Sunday. The most important thing was that communion was taken.

This time when I got baptized, the pastor said, "In the name of the Father, and of the Son and of the Holy Ghost, in Jesus Name" before putting his hand over my mouth and taking me under the water. I didn't feel any different. I didn't speak in tongues. I still believed what I believed when I was seven. Nothing changed except my outward appearance. The women said I wasn't filled with the Holy Ghost because I wasn't speaking in tongues yet. It didn't matter that I believed in Jesus. If they didn't hear me speak, there was no witness. So to them I didn't have the Holy Ghost and they said as much.

I'd managed to keep the rape from memory the next four years. I went on with my life staying busy with school, work and church while also trying to manage health issues of anemia and endometriosis. By then, my doctor told me that I'd probably never have children. I had to have a few surgeries to minimize constant pain and excessive bleeding. I still hadn't remembered the rape. I'd successfully stuffed it until the movie. My friend took me to see the movie, "What's Love Got to Do with It?"

Then it happened - the rape scene, the brutal, horrific rape scene. I freaked out right in the movie theater. I froze and then I cried uncontrollably until I was escorted out. My friend sat with me in the car silently and waited until I was able to calm myself down. I apologized for my embarrassing outburst and asked if he could take me home.

I remembered. I stared at myself in the mirror and remembered. I couldn't say it out loud, but I remembered. I was raped. I was blamed in a prayer to God for being raped. Minister James told God it was my fault he raped me. I remember the name calling. I remembered and I didn't know what to do with it. I couldn't tell anybody. I didn't want anybody to know. I was too ashamed. I was too angry. I was filled with overwhelming sadness. I felt dirty and thought going to church and praying to God would erase all of it. I thought church would make it better. I was looking for Him and desperately needing His help. I was looking to find Him from people who said they knew how to find Him. I was looking to find Him in a Bible I tried to understand in Sunday school and Bible classes.

Follow me as I follow Christ! That's what I heard. That's what I tried to do. What people, especially leaders, did and said mattered. My attempting to follow them as they followed Christ became a daunting task. I tried harder. I needed to be clean again. But, Jesus Christ became as they were to me: mean, untrustworthy, abusive and unloving. Who I was and what I was supposed to be got all tangled up in the confusion of religion and legalism. What I did became who I was.

Being born into the world comes with automatically knowing how to sin, but not automatically knowing how to be like Jesus. (Psalm 51: 5-6) said so. As a babe in Christ, I learned how to walk, talk, eat and grow up spiritually from pastors, leaders, and living epistles - believers. How shall they hear without a preacher? How shall they preach except they be sent? (Romans 10: 14-15) I didn't know how to interpret that scripture yet. Like so many others, I heard it quoted from the pulpit, but didn't know how to discern who was sent by God to be a preacher.

What if they get it wrong? In many ways, they did. What if they dropped me? In many ways, they did. What if they starved me? In many ways, they did. What if they fed me the wrong food? Yep, that happened too. What if they left me to figure it out for myself? Some of them did that. In the natural, it would be called child abuse. Neglected and abused children are protected by Human Services. They protect them from unfit parents. What happens when abuse and neglect happens in church? What happens to the spiritually abused and neglected babes? Who protects them?

Who was there to protect me from abusive, negligent leaders? No one was there. I was abandoned and unloved. I needed acceptance and love. The church was telling me I wasn't going to receive what I needed until I did all of the things that would warrant love. They expected me to change first instead of loving me into change. I jumped through all of the hoops they put in front of me. I'd been reading the Bible for years, but didn't understand most of what I was reading. I was told to read the Bible for myself. I was told I needed a teacher or pastor to teach me what the Bible meant. When I went with what I was taught, then I got blamed for being the victim of what I was taught.

CHAPTER **10**

Marriage and Divorce

1993-2002

I MET THE man who would be my husband in the late fall of 1991. I'd never met anyone like him. He was different than the other guys I knew. He was mild mannered and laid back with a healthy sense of humor, and deeply religious. We were friends, real friends. He made me laugh. Laughter was not one of my strong suits. It was a difficult task for anyone to accomplish, making me laugh, but he quickly mastered it.

We dated a few years. The longer we dated, the more it felt more like we were family, brother and sister. Throughout the years of dating, we stayed celibate. We wanted to live saved and free of sexual sin. But, if I'm honest, I didn't feel a spark anyway. I thought sex was overrated since I'd never experienced anything real before. Looking back, in retrospect, I didn't know much about relationships.

He was apostolic (Jesus only). I'd heard about the religion from other people, how they baptized in Jesus' name only, instead of the Father, Son, and Holy Spirit. I never understood the difference because I always thought God and Jesus were the same. He was born and raised into the religion. When we started talking about marriage, it was a given that I'd leave my current church and join the Apostolic church to be with him.

MARRIAGE AND DIVORCE

My pastor wasn't happy and said as much. "Don't go following in behind that man. I don't like him. There's something about him that's just not right." That's all he said. He didn't say what wasn't right. He didn't say what would happen if I followed him. He didn't tell me whatever it was he saw. I couldn't hear him because I couldn't get past the fact that he wasn't really nice to his own wife. I couldn't see past the obvious lack of love between them. I'd seen too much inconsistency to hear his warnings.

I didn't know at the time I was supposed to look past his faults and hear his shepherd's heart. I didn't know anything about a shepherd's heart or if he had one. I listened to him preach, watched him outside of the pulpit and got thrown off. I didn't see the connection between what I was hearing and what I was seeing. I didn't realize despite his position, my pastor was a man who knew men. As a man, he didn't like what he saw in the man I was about to marry.

I didn't listen. I went on to follow my fiancé to the new apostolic church. I went on to try to become "apostolic." I tried to conform to this religious community with all of its rules. Just like the other religions, they also had their own ideas about holiness and how to reach Heaven. Once again, I worked to be a better believer by attempting to follow the rules. The way the previous pastor baptized was sufficient enough to not do it again.

We went through what was considered marriage counseling. It was one day and only involved a series of questions like: Do you all have a job? Are you both saved? Are you both filled with the Holy Ghost? How long did you date? What are your goals for the near future? Children? How many? That was it. That was the extent of the marriage counseling.

It rained. Our wedding day started and ended with consistent rain. The rain would be a prophetic warning of what would be my married

TORN BIBLE

life. By the end of the reception, a new family member said to me, "Call me whenever you need to talk." I stared in disbelief. Need? Why would I need to call her? The look in her eyes was one of pity and worry. It was a look she knew I'd identify with, sooner, rather than later. I felt a wave of emotion. It was a sense of dread. It was another kind of grief.

As I watched her walk away, I felt the same sick feeling in my stomach. The feeling of nausea I'd felt when my Grandma died. This time it was me who'd died another death, the fourth being that day. The first three deaths I didn't have a name for. I didn't know it was death. I didn't know it was grief. I just knew something deep inside of me was dark and empty. It was the same feeling I had standing in the doorway of the sanctuary getting ready to walk down the aisle.

Just two hours earlier, I had a brief moment of what I thought was fear. I felt a strong desire to turn around and run out the door. I ignored it and chalked it up to wedding jitters. After her invitation to call, I knew it was much more than wedding jitters. But, it was too late. I'd already said I do. I didn't know what I said I do to. But, it would take eight years to get to, I don't.

"You look tired," Pastor said.

"I am," I answered, slouched in an oversized chair with one arm holding my chin up. "I can't do this anymore. I know what the Bible says in (Malachi 2:16) about God hating divorce. I've heard it quoted a million times, but I just can't, even if I don't have the grounds. It's not like I caught him cheating on me. I'm sorry pastor. I'll just have to do it and repent later. If I go to hell for divorcing, oh well."

He chuckled a little while he pulled his chair from behind his desk. He positioned it right in front of me. After sitting down and leaning in closer, he said, "No one has to tell you what you already know,

Sharon. You don't have to catch him doing anything. There are more ways to commit adultery than sleeping with another woman and I think we both know what those are."

I knew what I was thinking, what I knew, but until that moment, I didn't know he knew what I was thinking and knew. I didn't know he was thinking the same thing I was thinking. "Besides, you couldn't have known the kind of hell you'd end up in. All the things you've been dealing with are more than what many people in a marriage have been through in the short time you've been married. The Bible says God hates divorce because it's such a mess. It's a tearing apart. It's a death. Jesus said in (Matthew 19: 8-9) that divorce is permissible in case of adultery or you could interpret it to mean sexual immorality. Why? It's a break in covenant. Listen, God is for marriage, not mess, and what you have is a mess. You're not here in my office trying to get out of your marriage after a year or two of not even trying. You've been in it for eight years now. You've tried to do everything I've counseled you to do. You've even gone to see a professional marriage counselor."

He sat back in his chair and exhaled. He continued. "Sharon, you can't fix this by yourself. So, you have my permission to get the divorce."

I sat up in my chair and said, "Really, and I'm not going to hell?"

He laughed again, but I was serious.

"No. Divorce is not the unpardonable sin."

I walked out of that final counseling session feeling like I finally had hope for my future.

I thought no one could see the scars I had from the emotional, verbal and mental abuse I was experiencing. I didn't have words to describe body shaming, being reminded of how I didn't know how men were because my dad wasn't around and didn't want me, being reminded that I was from a single parent home and didn't know how to be a good wife, being reminded that no one would believe me because I was "unstable."

I couldn't describe doors slamming, abandonment, constant silent treatments, analyzing everything I said, and constantly hearing that I'm not sexy. I didn't know how to describe the knots I had in my stomach, the terror, suffocation, and walking on egg shells in my own home, trying to keep the peace and not say too much to avoid another fight. I couldn't describe being told "you're on medication, and so what you're feeling is not true. You're just imagining things. I didn't say that. I didn't take your keys. You heard wrong. You're too sensitive. You shouldn't wear your feelings on your sleeves. You're just weak. You can't divorce me because you don't have grounds. You can't prove anything. Remember, God hates divorce."

Some of the "church" women even told me what I was experiencing wasn't abuse. "Girl, I don't see one scar on you. That's not abuse." Or, "I don't care whatever you call it, he's saved right? I mean, if he's saved then God can change him. The Bible says the unsaved spouse is sanctified by the saved spouse. So, even if he isn't acting like the man God called him to be, you still have to submit to him. You need to be a good wife and cover him in prayer. He's a good man. He's in church. He knows the way. Just pray." I've heard it all.

In the meantime I was saying, "Yeah, but isn't it his job to cover me? He doesn't sleep in the bed with me. He hardly touches me. Sometimes, when I wake up in the middle of the night, he's not home. He doesn't want me!" I was crying and pleading for help. I tried hard to communicate, but I didn't have a voice. I knew I didn't know a lot which was why I was asking other "Godly" married women for help.

What I got each time was, "just keep praying." What was required of me kept flashing like a big red neon light, SUBMIT, SUBMIT, and SUBMIT some more. I was over it! I was done praying and I was done submitting.

I separated from him a few times, but went back because, well, "God hates divorce, right?" It's what I constantly heard in church and in my house. Who was I kidding? I literally hated him. I really hated him. I wasn't good at pretending everything was okay when it wasn't. I didn't have a poker face. What you saw is what you got from me. I was severely depressed, angry, enraged, and suicidal all at the same time. I knew that if I stayed in the marriage, someone was going to die, him or me.

I had to decide that I wasn't going to continue to go through the rules and regulations of marriage with no benefits. I was tired of feeling like a whore in my marriage. I was married for years, but I'd never experienced real love making. I never experienced intimacy. Each encounter was only a reminder of the sexual abuse I'd experienced prior to marriage. I felt like an actress in a bad pornography flick.

I made the decision that I wasn't going to be married in name and appearance only. I was too young to act like an old woman who was perfectly fine with a loveless, sexless marriage. I didn't want to be miserable. I didn't want to sleep in separate rooms for the rest of my life. There was absolutely no incentive for me to be married!

I wasn't being loved like Christ loved the church and gave Himself for it, all the while trying to be the submissive wife. I wasn't being cared for. The decision he made to quit his job when I'd just had a baby and couldn't work, left me not trusting him ever again to provide for me and our son. My patience was gone. I couldn't let another woman tell me, "You can't have everything. You're asking for too much. Marriage is hard work and it takes time."

Nope, my very life depended upon me leaving. And yet again, he was another man I couldn't count on to love me or provide for me. I made a vow to myself that I'd never trust another man to do anything for me ever again.

I resented the times I had to hurry up and heal from the multiple surgeries I'd had to go back to work because I was too afraid he would quit another job and we wouldn't have any money to pay the bills. When Jeremy was just a few days old and I had postpartum depression, instead of helping me, he berated me and ignored me when I asked that he not feed the baby apple sauce too soon. I became increasingly enraged and felt deceived.

I'd married someone who clearly didn't want to be married to me, but perhaps hoped that marrying me would cure whatever ailed him. I assumed he was fine with being married for years under a cloud of deceit. I wasn't okay with living in deception. It felt like I was a cover up, a smoke screen, someone to marry instead of burn in the most abominable way. I admit I didn't know much about love, but I knew enough to know this wasn't love.

I was a mess. By the time my marriage was near its end, I was sick and needy. I needed understanding and love. I couldn't understand if he was so miserable with me, which he often said, why did he even want to stay married to me? If I was too needy, too much work, too depressed, too unstable, then, why? What was it all for? I didn't understand and I wasn't interested in staying to find out.

Going through the divorce shed light on who was really for me and who was not for me. People I thought I could count on decided friendship wasn't worth continuing beyond my marriage. To them, I was someone's wife and that warranted a relationship. Without that title, that position, that status in church, I was nobody worth knowing as a single woman. I was still a mother, but a single mother. This meant the married mothers didn't see a need to continue sharing recipes, home decorating tips, or stories of little league games and school plays. I was in the same church, but suddenly found myself very much alone.

Those married women who prayed with me, talked and gave advice to me about my marriage and parenting, were now squeezing and pulling their husbands' arms closer to them when I walked past, as if I was suddenly attracted to and wanted them. Surrogate fathers for my son suddenly stopped calling and spending time with him. So, not only did folks end relationships with me, but my son also. I experienced the mess the process of divorce brought. I went through threats of losing custody citing mental incompetence, threatening phone calls of "If you do this, then I'll make sure you pay," vicious name calling, some of which my five year old heard, causing me to try and get restraining orders. I had to let family members, doctors and my therapist know what was going on, just in case.

My therapist assured me that in order for my ex-husband to make the case for mental incompetence, he'd have to prove it. He said, "The lawyers will start digging and I'd have to testify to your mental capacity. So, you don't have anything to worry about. Mental illness does not equal crazy. You're sick, but, you're functioning. You're maintaining a good job and you're more than capable of raising your son. If I didn't think so, I'd say so."

I understood what battered women went through because I was that woman and I was going through it. My therapist informed me that I was a battered wife a year or two prior to filing for divorce. He looked me in my eyes and said, "You do know you're a battered woman, right?" I was bewildered. He seemed to be looking right through me, into my soul. "I don't mean to alarm you, Sharon, but do you know what a battered woman syndrome is?"

Moving my head from side to side I said, "No."

He went on to explain. "It's a mental disorder that develops in victims of domestic violence as a result of serious, long-term abuse. That abuse isn't isolated to physical violence. In many ways, mental, emotional, sexual and verbal abuse is just as bad, if not worse."

I experienced firsthand how difficult it was to get the protection needed from law enforcement. I was told after the police listened to threatening phone messages, "Well, did he try and come to the house yet? You should change your locks."

"Yes sir. I did that already."

"That's good," he said, slightly shifting his body from one side to the other. Pausing for a few seconds, as if bracing himself for a reaction he'd seen from women like me many times before, he said, "Well Ma'am, it doesn't appear from the messages we've heard, he gave any plausible threat of bodily harm." Unfortunately, all we can do is have you fill out a police report and paperwork documenting what happened. Oh, and try and save those messages too. This way, we'll have a paper trail."

I didn't know whether to cry or throw a complete tantrum. I couldn't believe what I was hearing. "This is some kind of joke, right? So, you're saying to me that if I come in with a black eye or end up in the hospital with busted ribs or something like that, then you'll be able to do something?"

"I'm afraid so, Ma'am. We'll need to establish a pattern."

I had no words. While the officer was still talking, I turned toward the door, walked out of the police station and got in my car, a brand new 1998 Gold Chevy Cavalier. I bought the car in the fall of 1997, six months after my son was born. I taught myself how to drive so I wouldn't have to continue taking my newborn on public transportation to doctor's appointments, stores, or visits with family, and so I wouldn't have to keep hearing how dependent I was on him. He keyed my car because he was angry. I got in that car and cried my eyes out because, once again, I had no one to protect me, not even the ones sworn to serve and protect.

Part 3
Mental Illness

CHAPTER 11

Clinical Depression

Major Depressive Disorder Diagnosis 2001

2001 WAS THE year I was diagnosed with Clinical Depression. Doctor Chad explained it more in depth as a combination of Major Depressive, Anxiety and Post Traumatic Stress Disorders. I was thirty three years old. Doctor Chad, my therapist, said I had a chemical imbalance in my brain which worsened over the years. He said my brain worked differently. He said the multiple sexual traumas, stresses and abuses I'd suffered since childhood only intensified the illness. He helped me discover the pattern. My birth resulting from an affair, the guilt I carried from Deacon Jackson's wife dying allegedly because I was born, the dead man in the casket, the fear, the molestation, the rape, the church abuse, and the nightmare of a marriage.

He immediately prescribed medication along with psychotherapy. He said it's a serious mental illness that affected my feelings, thoughts, social and possibly daily functions. He said I'd experienced horrific things with greater depth. As a result of my sensitive personality along with everything else, I felt things deeply and with greater intensity. They were the same words Mama used to describe me when I was much younger.

After going over my history from birth to early adulthood as well as the checklist, he determined I'd had some form of mental illness for decades. The checklist: little or no interest or pleasure in doing things, easily startled, feelings of sadness and hopeless, insomnia, sleeping too much, poor appetite, over eating, always tired, trouble concentrating, anxiety and suicidal. He had every box checked. Dr. Chad was the only psychologist in all of those years of going to doctors who did the checklist. He was the only one who diagnosed me properly.

In the 1970s, 80s and 90s, mental illness was not something that was discussed or even acknowledged within the Black community. It was definitely unheard of in the Black church. In the Black Pentecostal churches, mental illness was nothing more than demonic possession or oppression. Mama always knew something was wrong and tried her best to get me help and still, no one diagnosed me. Mama did all the praying and talking in the early years. She was my only counselor and intercessor.

I learned as much as I could about the illness. I read books. I asked a lot of questions and talked with my doctors and therapists. I told them I didn't want to be known as a sick person. I didn't want to be a collection of symptoms. I didn't want to be a medicated shell of a person. I wanted to be treated like a real person who was getting the help I needed. They all agreed and treated me like the intelligent human being I was.

I spoke with the pastor and shared with him what my therapists and doctors shared with me. He was extremely supportive and encouraged me to take whatever medication was prescribed. He was intelligent and had a good understanding about the illness. He was a spirit filled man of wisdom who didn't reduce me to a demonic oppressed woman of faith. He assured me that it didn't mean I had to be on medication forever. His counsel and prayers gave me a little comfort. I told Mama. She understood, but didn't want me to be medicated. She never said so, but I think she thought I'd become addicted

TORN BIBLE

or something. She didn't want me to be all loopy. She told me to pray and keep on praying. I did.

It appeared my husband and the person who I thought was a close friend didn't seem as understanding. My husband and my frenemy didn't understand that loving and having compassion for me would've been the best support they could've given me. Instead of covering me, I was analyzed. What I said was analyzed. What I did was analyzed. My plight grew worse. My frenemy mocked me. She told me I should pretend I was okay so no one at church would think I was crazy. She had no problems calling and telling me when I didn't play the role correctly. "Yeah, someone called me and said you were acting a little different today." I had nothing to say. What was I supposed to say? I was different.

I had a meltdown in the choir stand on a Sunday morning. I'm not sure what song was being sung or what the sermon was about. I just cried uncontrollably. I was on the floor between the pews on the second row of soprano section with my hands over my head screaming and crying. My fellow sopranos looked. No hugs and no kneeling down next to me. They just looked. I can't say whether they prayed. But, at that moment, I needed help. I needed love. I needed compassion. I didn't need silent prayers.

Maybe I was acting too unseemly. Maybe they were thrown off by my behavior because I've always been quiet and reserved. My outburst, tears, on the floor sitting upright with my knees to my chest and hands over my head, confused them. My mind drew a blank. I'm not sure how I got up or what happened after that. I do remember the phone call I got that evening.

My frenemy called. The conversation went something like,

"Are you okay? I mean, I only called because Brenda was concerned about you. She asked me if you were okay."

I couldn't believe my ears. She wanted to know if I was okay. Really? Clearly, I wasn't okay.

"What did you say to her?" I asked.

"Well, I just told her to pray for you. Sharon, did you take your medicine? I mean, because if you were taking it you probably wouldn't have acted that way."

My response to her was, "Click." It was over. She was over.

The next Sunday I went to church. I sat in the audience instead of singing in the choir. The previous Sunday was my last Sunday singing. When the altar call was made, I got up and got in line for prayer. The ministers and altar workers stood across the front and prayed for people one by one. The minister that would've prayed for me when it was my turn walked away from the altar and went out a side door when she saw I would be the next person for her to pray for. She clearly didn't want to pray for me.

Maybe she knew about my illness. Maybe she saw me have a meltdown in the choir stand the previous Sunday. Maybe my husband or one of his minister friends told her I was crazy. All I knew was, she saw me waiting in line and she didn't want to pray for me. I was hurt. I was humiliated. I was frustrated. I didn't want prayer anymore. I didn't want another prayer warrior or minister to reject praying for me. I turned around and went back to my seat. My faith, what little I had, was failing.

I'm sure there were those who could see that something was wrong with me, but didn't say anything. I wanted to believe someone was praying for me. I wanted to believe not everyone at church was just plain cruel. For every church member who walked on the other side of the church when they saw me coming or the mother who gave me the side eye after possibly having a conversation with someone, there were members who cared. I wanted to believe.

The horrible mistreatment and rejection outweighed the good. I was still trying to press on. I was still trying to work in ministry. I was still trying to be faithful, even though my faith was steadily failing. I started the Ministers in Training program. I was assigned to different tasks throughout the church. I wasn't singing in the choir anymore, but was working in the prayer room. I was working in the baptismal room. I was working in the Girls' Ministry. I was working. I had faith for other people, but not really for myself. I'd prayed for other people and watched God work on their behalf. I was working until a meeting I had with a few elders who were over the Ministers in Training program.

I needed prayer and I told them so. Before the meeting got started, I asked.

"I have a prayer request. I need-"

One of the elders interrupted, "You're a minister in training, aren't you? You can pray for yourself." Another one said, "We don't have time for victim mentalities. No one has time to hold your hand. If you want to be a minister, you're going to have to toughen up."

I paused. My heart immediately started to ache. I looked them in the eyes one by one. I looked to see if I saw anything that resembled care. I looked for love. I looked for compassion. I looked for the why of ministry. Instead, I saw judgment. I saw pious attitudes. I saw smugness.

They knew. Someone told them. Was it my now ex-husband? Was it my ex-frenemy? I saw it in their eyes. I saw that they didn't know what to do with me. I saw how they didn't know how to treat me. I saw what I didn't want to become. I felt as if I was in a court of religious law, before three self – righteous legalistic judges, being sentenced to life in the prison of cold hearted hypocrisy. There was no need for a meeting. I said, "Thank you for your time." I made my escape. I quickly walked out.

CHAPTER **12**

I Stopped

I Couldn't Heal As I went, So I Stopped

I STOPPED. I quit. They didn't want me to be a victim or have a victim mentality. I was and I did. I didn't want to, but.... They wanted me to be tough. I wasn't. They wanted me to pretend that I was okay. I wasn't. They wanted me to wear a mask. I couldn't.

If being a minister meant I could no longer be in need of prayer, ask for someone else to pray for me, need a word, need a hug, or be human, then I didn't want to be a minister. If it meant I had to pretend to be strong when I wasn't, then I couldn't be a minister. So I stopped. I stopped working in ministry. I slowly stopped going to Bible class, prayer services, and finally Sunday services. I just stopped.

I began to journal. I talked to God. I talked to myself. I wrote poetry. I wrote prayers. I didn't know how to be spiritually correct. I just wrote. I couldn't go back to church. I was tired. I was sick. I didn't want to pretend there was nothing wrong when there was. I did all I could. I listened when the praise leader said, "Lift your hands. Give a sacrifice of praise. Sing your way out of depression." I sang. I lifted my hands. I praised. I was still sad, still depressed, still jumpy, and still anxious.

I obeyed when the preacher said, "Tell your neighbor, I'm coming out week after week. Leap for joy. Turn around three times, and on the third turn, say I'm free." I talked to my neighbor. I said I'm coming out when I was still in. I leaped. I turned around three times. I said I'm free. I didn't feel free. I listened when scriptures were quoted. I read my Bible. I believed what I read. But, I was told I didn't have faith because no Holy Ghost filled believer should have a mental Illness. I was tired of being treated like a project. I was tired of people giving me a "word," and practicing spiritual gifts on me. I was tired of being watched.

Church antics made it harder for me to get better. It was pressure I didn't need. I needed God's help, but I didn't have the energy to do religious acrobatics. I looked forward to going to see Dr. Chad more often. When I walked into his office, I felt safe. His office was filled with shelves of Bibles and books. His walls were decorated with mountains and water paintings. His furniture was comfortable cushioned chairs and a couch that swallowed me when I sat down. His office provided something I didn't get at church. Peace. He was peaceful and calming. When he prayed, his prayers were simple and faith filled. His words were uncomplicated. He sat in his chair and calmly talked with God about me.

I didn't feel pressured to say anything. My silence was acceptable. My tears weren't judged. Dr. Chad guided me in conversation. I told him I stopped going to church. He didn't say the blood of Jesus. He didn't rebuke me. He didn't say I was going to hell.

He said, "Okay."

"Aren't you going to ask me why?"

"If you want to tell me, I'll listen."

I told him, "I didn't feel safe at church. I couldn't pretend anymore."

TORN BIBLE

"Pretend how?" he asked.

"Pretend that I'm okay when I'm not."

"Why would you have to pretend?"

I'm sure he knew why, but wanted to hear me say it. He was sure of his gift of discerning, word of knowledge, or whatever. He didn't need to practice his gifts on me.

Dr. Chad talked to me with compassion. He asked me if I was okay. He asked me how I was feeling and really wanted an answer.

"Has the medication been making you feel sick? How is your appetite? Are you sleeping okay?

Are you having trouble praying?"

"Praying?" I asked.

"Yes, praying."

"I'm not sure." I said. "I mostly journal and I say things like, dear God and God what do you think about this and God how do you feel about this?"

He said. "That's praying."

I was partly relieved and partly confused. "It is?"

"Of course," he answered. "The psalms can be considered journals, poetry, songs, most importantly, prayers."

It was refreshing to be able to trust a man, a middle aged man with dirty blond hair and blue eyes, and a man who wanted nothing sexual from me. Dr. Chad was the only man I could trust to be transparent. I was safe with him. I was safe to say what I was thinking no matter how off putting or confusing. I told him how I wanted to die. I told him how I wanted my now ex-husband to die. I didn't like how angry I'd become or bitter and how enraged I'd become.

"Why won't he just die already?" I'd ask.

"I guess because, It's not his time."

"Well, then, I want to die."

"I believe it's not your time either. You don't really want to die at this point in your life, Sharon. You just want the pain to go away. If you can't find the will to get better and live for yourself, do it for your son."

"Do it for my son." That's what I told myself when I wanted to give up again. My son really kept me going. Dr. Chad helped me see how important it was to keep working hard to heal. He reasoned with my heart. He reminded me of what could possibly happen to my son if I didn't survive. What would happen if I acted on my feelings of hate and anger? Who would get custody of my son? My ex-husband had brought out the worse in me. He stressed it was imperative that I be healed because my son's health and life depended on it.

CHPATER **13**

Church Killed Me!

2005-2010

WHAT WAS MEANT to lead me to God nearly destroyed me. Some of these churches cost more than what I could afford to pay. The church took all that was in me and left me sicker than I was before. There were times I attempted to find another hospital (church) to heal me from damage done at the last hospital (church). I was desperate enough to crawl through crowds of doubters, judgmental attitudes, rejection, religious minded people and abusive leaders to get to Jesus. Desperation caused me to press through smelling bad, looking bad, and being treated like trash. I had a choice to bleed to death or crawl and fight my way to Jesus. In doing so, I was finding my life. Except, the process of finding my life and Jesus would take years. I'd been so hurt, so offended, and so disappointed by church people and church leaders who I thought cared about me. I expected people in the church to love me with what the Bible called "love."

One incident that changed my life and how I viewed "the saints" in the worst possible way happened at the Church Of God In Christ. I went to a choir retreat the church sponsored. I was so excited because I was looking forward to growing closer to God. According to the announcements made, a retreat was a great way to quiet everything down to spend quality time to pray and hear from God. I wanted Him so badly that I was willing to try anything. It was my very first retreat. However, I didn't bank on being rejected to pray.

A group of people decided to get together in one of their rooms to pray together. I overheard them planning and asked if I could come too. I didn't really know how to pray, not like I heard in church, but I wanted to learn. To my amazement, I was told by the young lady planning the prayer meeting that I could not come because she didn't want to hinder the "move of God." I immediately deflated like a balloon. This prominent "holy" member of the Church Of God In Christ had rejected me from learning how to pray. I was rejected from prayer.

I didn't know what to say. I just knew how I felt. I knew having the Holy Ghost was a big deal and speaking in tongues were a sure sign you had "it." Well, I hadn't done that yet, which to them meant I didn't have "it" yet. Maybe that's why I was rejected, because I didn't have "it" yet. I didn't know that much about God to separate how He felt about me versus how His people felt about me. So, in that moment, she represented Him. What it said to me again was I wasn't worthy or good enough to talk to God.

I was left to fill in the blanks and all the words I used to fill in the blanks came from my pain and what God's people said about me. She said, "If I came to prayer I would hinder the move of God." How could I possibly hinder the move of God? If I didn't have His Spirit, what spirit did I have? If it's the wrong spirit, how was I supposed to get the right spirit? Why couldn't I pray with them?

I was taught by word and experience that the way to holiness had everything to do with how I looked. I looked through the Bible to support their argument of dress in correlation to holiness, but I didn't see anything about it. As a woman, I had to make sure I didn't wear things that brought attention to me or was tempting to the men of God. That's what the older women said. I went from one situation to a whole new level of bondage. Being subjected to those kinds of "man-made rules" didn't help my already damaged life. To come from a place of sexual abuse at the hands of "men of God," to be told that if I wore long skirts, take off my makeup and jewelry, then the "men of God" wouldn't be tempted and I'd be free of further sexual assault.

God has a way of keeping you even when you think you don't want to be kept. I wanted to run as far away as I could get. In some ways I did run. In many ways, I was gone, just not physically gone. What happens when you don't know how to manage your feelings and emotions? What happens when you're not thinking the way you should think and don't have the help you need? What if you do lose your mind? I really thought I'd finally lost my mind and maybe I did.

Church was supposed to give me life. It gave me death. I thought I could forget how I was conceived. I thought I could forget about the dead man and the fear that came with me being placed inside his casket. I thought I could forget about the molestation. I thought I could forget about the rape. I thought I could forget about the abusive marriage. I thought being in church, working in church would help me heal and live. I was wrong. I died instead.

How could I think the very place I experienced trauma could help me? How could I possibly think the place where every man I had horrible experiences with, could help me? Every one of these men had something to do with ministry and leadership in the church. How did I think the place where women taught other women that a man's lust problem had everything to do with her appearance, help me? Paul instructed older women in (Titus 2:3-5) to teach younger women. But, some of them taught based on how they interpreted the scripture, with a little tradition, culture and preferences mixed in. Those interpretations, traditions, cultures, and preferences didn't help me heal. They made my life worse. They pushed me further into depression and hopelessness.

I was beyond exhausted. I couldn't please God and the church. Being "holy" was too hard. I was mentally and emotionally not well. I knew it. Going to church and trying to survive church only added to my mental and emotional stress. After constantly hearing what a woman should do, how a woman should look and act, and her "role" as a wife, I'd had it. I didn't have any more strength to keep "doing things." I didn't want to hear another church mother give excuses for why men acted the way that they did. Not another, "He's just being a man. They just can't help themselves. Don't show too much because you don't want to be a stumbling block. You got to pray and keep on praying." Yeah, I was done.

Older women teaching young women to stay in abuse is foolish. Teaching young women to continue sleeping with their husbands and knowing he's cheating on her or treating her like the bottom of his shoe, isn't wise. It's foolish. It's sexual abuse. Training young women in the church to keep quiet when she knows her husband is causing chaos in the home is foolish. I was told to do all of this by older women who'd been married for decades. Some of these women lived with constant repeat offenders of abuse and adultery. They taught other women to do the same in the spirit of submissiveness and humility.

But for me, silence equals acceptance. I refused to continue accepting just anything. Continuing to do "wifely duties" without confronting issues and demanding respect is foolish. The strength of a woman was never supposed to be measured by how much pain she can endure. I said as much and got rebuked for it. Adding culture, traditions and preferences to scriptures about anything, especially being a "Godly" woman, nearly ruined my life.

They taught by their actions, or lack thereof, that the Holy Ghost was gender specific. The over emphasis on the Holy Ghost being a keeper for women, but not men was overbearing. A man got a pass on controlling his own body in holiness and honor, (1 Thessalonians

4:3-8), because it was the woman's job to keep her and him, "holy." A woman's attire in "holiness" was bondage. The long thrift store skirts, oversized blouses and jackets were meant to cover a woman's shape in hopes of curing lust. Outdated hairstyles and makeup free faces were in my opinion, attempts to make us look as unattractive as possible. I didn't understand why some men in the church were so easily enticed. I didn't understand the hierarchy and misogynistic mentality in the church. I couldn't be responsible for a man's mistreatment of me anymore. I couldn't carry the weight of keeping myself, "covered" to be and feel safe.

I wasn't going to another convocation, PAW convention, women's conference, women's retreat, marriage seminar, women's Bible study, nothing. I wasn't reading another book on how to be a praying wife or a virtuous woman. The next time someone suggested reading another how-to book on Christian womanhood, my response will be "I will when somebody comes up with how to be a praying husband or a Godly man." Until then, take your books and shelve them.

I spent Sunday mornings in bed with the television watching me. I slept. It was the first time ever I wasn't spending sun up to sun down in church. Nobody called to say I miss you, I'm praying for you. I got phone calls from people trying to guilt me into going to church.

"If you can go to work every day, you can go to church. You're just making excuses. You just want to be a victim. You don't want God, because if you did, you'd come to church. You don't love the Lord."

I couldn't deal with the constant religious bullying and nagging. I needed peace. I needed to get well.

For the first time in my life I understood why people backslide. I understood why people didn't like going to church. It wasn't because they didn't want to know God. It wasn't because most people didn't believe there's a God. I think they do. It wasn't because they didn't want to learn how to live better lives. I think they did. Most people genuinely wanted to be right and do right. They just couldn't get past some of the people, their judgmental attitudes, and their coldness. They couldn't get past pastors who didn't care. They couldn't get past all the extra add-ons in addition to the Bible. Like me, they probably couldn't deal with the pressure of church. It's just too hard to do all the stuff and be a hypocrite.

I experienced firsthand how mean spirited some of the "saints" could be and I was tired of it. Their arguments were irrational. Going to church for tradition didn't work with me. Going because I needed to fellowship with the "saints" didn't work with me either. I didn't need to be part of another social organization with no power.

I needed help. I needed love. I was needy. Neediness and holiness didn't go together. Neediness and church didn't go together. I heard too much of, "Aren't you over that yet. Why aren't you healed yet? You need to have thick skin. You cry too much. You have a calling on your life, but something's not right in your head."

I was angry, hurt, tired, wounded, fed up, and just pissed off. I wasn't going back. There was no reason for me to go back to church. I was bewildered about church. I was overwhelmed with church.

I changed everything to fit in church. I was looking for Jesus. I needed Jesus. I did everything I was told to do to find Him. I tarried and got tongue tied. I prayed. I went to service several times a week. I read my Bible and learned their interpretations taught from the pulpit. I hadn't learned how to study to show myself approved yet. My faith or lack thereof, came from hearing the Word of God from a preacher. The Word of God wasn't my problem. It was the preacher's interpretation of it. It was the way scriptures were taken out of context. I wouldn't figure that out until much later in life.

TORN BIBLE

I became who they said I was supposed to become - a woman of God. I took off stuff. I put on stuff. I was never myself. I didn't know myself. I wasn't sure if I ever really knew me. Who I was supposed to be died when I was ten years old in my pastor's office. I worked to be loved and accepted. I worked to be a good wife and mother to the best of my ability. I worked and got tired.

CHAPTER **14**

Justin

THERE WAS SOMETHING about him, something that gave me a sense of excitement. Justin was the first person who greeted me when I started my new job. He was helpful and kind. The more we worked together, the more I grew to admire and respect him. I looked forward to going to work every day. His unorthodox way of working made the long days a lot less stressful.

Justin was tall and slightly thin, like a basketball player. He was intelligent and goal oriented. His style was a cross between bohemian and casual chic. His hair was just at his shoulders, neatly locked with perfect edges. He was earthy. He smoked weed and got drunk on weekends. He burned incense and liked African art and furniture. He believed Jesus was real. He believed Him to be God. He appreciated and admired creation. He wanted nothing to do with the church. He was perfect.

We were total opposites. I was a church girl who didn't go to church anymore. He was a renaissance man who was passionate about healthy living and vegetarian recipes. We built a relationship around exercise and eating right. I was newly divorced and overweight. Instead of body shaming me, something I was used to, he taught me all he knew about healthy living. He taught me what foods would be healthier to eat. He took walks with me. He listened to me and took interest in things I liked to do. I took interest in things he liked.

Justin wasn't like the suit wearing, Bible toting, scripture quoting, tongue talking, abusive church men I knew. He was different. He was sexy. He was honest. He didn't make empty promises. He didn't lie to me. He shared his relationship adventures with me. I didn't expect anything that resembled religious loyalty, exclusiveness, or covenant. I just wanted a friend, a friend who happened to be a man. I wanted to feel like a woman who wasn't a victim of sexual abuse with a mental health condition.

Months went by before I could tell him about the depression. I was afraid he'd think I was crazy. I was afraid he wouldn't want to see me again. I told him about my disaster of a marriage and how I didn't feel like a real woman. I told him I didn't feel that I'd ever been made love to. I finally got the courage to tell him about the depression while we cuddled and watched the movie, Baby Boy. Justin hated the movie. He lost interest after, as he put it, "Watching a grown ass man arguing with his mama about putting him out."

His disdain for the movie was yet another reason why I liked him. He was a real man. His response to my depressive condition made me fall for him even more.

"Yeah, well, are you getting better now?"

"Yes. The medication helps. I go to therapy once a week. That helps too."

"That's good. As long as it's helping you is all that matters. At least you're doing something about it. That's big. I'm proud of you for that."

He smiled at me and gently slid his hand around my waist. Wow. He was proud of me. I snuggled into his arms and positioned my head on his chest.

I couldn't believe he was that understanding. I waited to see if he was just being polite. I waited to see if he'd stop calling me or treat me different at work. The phone calls didn't stop. We kept going out for walks. We kept having deep philosophical conversations. He treated me like the intelligent educated woman I was. I appreciated his friendship. I looked forward to going to work every day because I knew he'd be there. I looked forward to sleeping with him on weekends because he was the first person ever with whom I actually experienced real intimacy.

I liked being in his apartment. His apartment was vintage and charming and fit in with the upscale neighborhood where he lived. Each time I walked in, I was welcomed by a mixture of soothing oils, candles and incense. I liked lying in his arms talking about goals and dreams. He listened as I went on and on about what I wanted to experience in life. He listened as I told him how much better I felt since I wasn't going to church and trying to live up to rules and regulations. For the first time in my life, I had pillow talk. For the first time in my life, sex didn't feel distant. He was present with me. It wasn't superficial, fake, or empty. I wasn't just a body. I mattered.

I mattered in the way he put his hand around my waist and pulled me close, and in the way he took my face in his hands and asked, "You okay?"

My answer was always, "Yes. I am now."

I was okay every time I was with him. The way I put my ear to his chest and listened to his heart beat, relaxed me. The rhythm in his breathing was meditation. I adored him.

TORN BIBLE

Our friendship went on for months. We worked together successfully. Neither one of us talked about our friendship with other friends or co-workers. We were strictly professional at work. Things were great between us, so I thought. We talked on the phone often, but conversations were starting to take an awkward turn. I talked more and he talked less. He'd listen to me say whatever I needed to say and then he'd abruptly say, "I have to go."

We'd never really argued about anything, which is why the last conversation we had hurt so much. He called to tell me he had something important to talk with me about.

"Sharon, I've been listening to you talk for a while now and it seems like you're trying to come over into my world instead of staying in your own world."

I was confused. "What?" I snapped.

"What I mean is, I really like you, but, I know who I am. I've noticed you're trying to fit into my world of living without church or God. You're pulling farther away from who you are."

"Who I am? What are you talking about?"

I was starting to feel the sting of rejection again. The more he talked, the angrier I became. He continued. "Look, the church is still in you or God or something. Anyway, you're trying to leave something that has you. Besides, the more time I spend with you, the more uncomfortable it is for me." "Is it what I told you about the depression?"

"No, not at all. I think it's more spiritual."

"Spiritual? Are you serious?"

"I know. Don't laugh," he said. "I feel like if I keep messing around with you, God will kill me. I think I need to end it."

"End it?" I yelled.

"Sharon, it's not you. I really care about you. It's God, I think. I know its God."

"God? God? Are you kidding me? Since when do you listen to God?"

"Since, I don't want to die."

"Wait. What?"

"Look, can we just be civil about this? I don't want to end as enemies."

"Oh, so, you just want to be friends without benefits?"

"Yes, if we can."

"Look, I have to go now. I'll call you later or something, if that's okay."

"Sure, of course it is."

I sat on the side of my bed staring off into space. I tried to fight back the tears that were welling up in my eyes. Like a tsunami, suddenly water was coming out of every hole in my face. I was devastated. I was furious, I was feeling overwhelming sadness. I was experiencing another loss. I wiped my eyes and nose with my sleeve.

I started rocking back and forth, seething with anger. I wanted to direct my out of control emotions at Justin, but I cared about him too much. I rehearsed what he said over and over again in my head.

"It's God."

He said God. I stood up and started throwing things and yelling at God as if He was standing in front of me.

"How could You do this to me? How could You take him away from me? Why can't I experience real love? How could You take the only man who saw me, who wanted me? I was safe with him. You don't want me to have a man to love me."

I went on and on, yelling and screaming at God until I wore myself out.

I woke up the next morning not realizing I'd fallen asleep the night before. I remembered throwing things and yelling at God, but not falling asleep. I sat up on the side of the bed and looked around at all the mess I'd made. I stared at it, before going in to check on Jeremy. He was still asleep. It was a Sunday morning. I walked through the house in a daze, periodically checking my phone for possible missed calls from Justin. I was hoping it was all a bad dream. I was hoping he'd call, say he made a mistake and didn't hear God after all. I was hoping he'd call and declare his love for me. My hopes were just hopes.

CHAPTER **15**

Something's on me

SOMETHING'S ON ME. That's what I told Kasey. Kasey was another therapist I had to get to know and trust when I was laid off my job. Dr. Chad was still my primary therapist, but only when I could afford to pay him out of pocket. In the meantime, I met with Kasey. She was a Christian therapist like Dr. Chad. Her degrees from Northwestern University and the University of Chicago were proudly displayed on her wall. Like him, she had a calm demeanor and a bright smile to boot. Her big green eyes sparkled brighter each time she gave a light grin. Her dark hair was cut into a short funky style that matched her choice of clothes. She looked to be in her late 30s, but I wasn't certain. She sat patiently the first day while I expressed my reservations of her. I told her it wasn't personal. She said she understood. She said she knew what it was like to start over.

She did the checklist too. She confirmed Dr. Chad's diagnosis, but added she didn't like labels. "We're not going to put a title on you. We're just going to talk. Is that okay with you?"

"Yes, that's fine."

She talked for weeks while I gave short responses.

"Yes. No. I'm not sure. Maybe."

After a month, I told her, "Something's on me."

She knew the right questions to ask. She didn't ask what because she knew I didn't know what.

Instead, she asked, "What does something feel like to you?"

"Dirty. Gross. I don't like it."

She nodded. "Do you feel like telling me what you've been up to lately?"

I answered, "I guess."

She waited through my long pause. "I haven't talked to God since I yelled at Him." I sighed.

"Why did you yell at Him?"

"He made Justin stop seeing me."

"I can see why that would make you angry. From what you told me last week, he seems like a really nice guy. We can talk about him if you want."

"No. I'm not ready to talk about him."

"That's okay," she answered. "So, you haven't written in your journal either?"

"No. I don't have anything to say."

"Did you think about what we discussed the last time you were here?"

"Yes. I don't think I'm ready to go back to church," I answered.

"Okay." She didn't press.

"Tell me about the something you think is on you."

I didn't know how to explain it, so I just told her what I'd been doing since breaking up with Justin and yelling at God.

"I started talking to this guy from the apostolic church I left. He called to see how I was doing and said he'd been missing me at church. He asked if I wanted to go out for coffee. At first it puzzled me because he'd never shown an interest in me before."

She listened attentively.

"Anyway, I went ahead and went with him for coffee. He wasn't really my type, but he seemed nice enough."

"We talked for several weeks on the phone, but the last conversation I had with him shook me." Kasey leaned her head to one side and waited for me to continue.

"He started talking about my depression. I asked him who told him. He said, "It doesn't matter who told me.""

I said, "It does matter. Now, who told you?"

Ignoring my demand for answers, he said, "Who do you think you're talking to like that?"

"Like what? I'm talking to you and I asked, who told you? I'm not understanding why this is so hard to figure out."

"Dang, if you really need to know, your so-called friend told me."

"No surprise there," I said under my breath.

"What?"

"Nothing."

"How did that make you feel?" Kasey asked.

"I felt betrayed all over again. Then he had the nerve to ask me out again."

"Really?"

"Yes."

I asked him, why did he want to go out with me?

He said, "I thought you could use some company. You know, a friend."

"What kind of friend?" I knew what he wanted by then, but I asked anyway.

"You know," he said.

Kasey nodded again. She knew what he wanted too.

"I don't know what happened to me Kasey. I just lost it. I snapped."

"What did you do?" She inquired.

"I attacked his manhood. I hurled insult after insult at him so fast he didn't know what to say.

I said, "I'm not even attracted to you. You're two feet tall and you're probably little anyway. Even if I wanted to have sex, it wouldn't be with you. You probably don't even know what to do. You probably wouldn't know how to keep your mouth shut either. You'd run to your church friends and tell them everything just like you called here telling me what you heard. You're a pathetic little man. I slammed the phone down."

"Wow," Kasey said. "You really said all of that?"

"Yep, and it felt good too. That's when I thought about it."

"Thought about what?"

"I thought about charging. If that's what was on me, all they saw, all any of them took or tried to take like the little man that called, they would have to pay me."

She sighed. She looked into my eyes. I looked into her eyes. I didn't flinch.

"Is that what you really want?"

I didn't answer her. I didn't know what I wanted. I only knew what I didn't want. I didn't want to be treated like a piece of meat anymore. If that's what they wanted, I would do that, but not without compensation.

Instead, I told her what I was going to do.

"I'm not going to be the weak sex victim anymore. I'm not going to be the weak little church woman who men can dominate. From now on, I'm doing the victimizing. I'm going to dominate. If that's what they want, they're going to pay dearly."

Our hour was up. Kasey scheduled a visit for the next two weeks. Before letting me go, she prayed. She never prayed at the end of a session, just the beginning. This time she prayed again.

"Father, I ask you to love on Sharon. Smother her with Your unconditional love. Let her know You're with her even when she doesn't think You are and even when she doesn't feel You. I rebuke the hand of the enemy that's trying hard to destroy her life. Lord, I pray You draw her back to You, in Jesus' name, Amen."

Her prayers were answered, but not before my need for tangible love gave way to rage and rebellion. I was headed down the road toward hatred of men and permanent distrust in God. My desire to trust Him and believe His love for me diminished with each passing day. I took it out on men. I tried to make them pay for it. They would pay for every other man who'd mistreated me.

I met another guy. I didn't remember his name. I guess because it was irrelevant. He was irrelevant. I saw him once or twice, maybe a few times. I made sure he had enough money for a nice dinner and jewelry or something I considered valuable. Each time, I left him in the middle of the night.

He'd ask me to stay and talk.

I'd say, "For what? I don't want to talk."

"Okay, I'll call you."

"Don't bother."

"What? Are you serious?"

"Yes." I rolled my eyes. "I thought you'd be happy to not have expectations from a woman. Why are you so shocked?"

He sat up in the bed and stared at me in disbelief. After getting dressed, he watched as I grabbed my purse and headed for the door.

"Hey! So, you're not going to say anything?"

I said, "Oh, yeah, bye."

He called anyway. The man whose name I couldn't remember. The man whose name I didn't want to remember. I answered without looking at my phone to see who was calling.

"Hello?"

"Well, hello beautiful."

"Who is this?"

"Oh, so now you don't know me?"

"I never knew you."

"You're really something, you know that?" I held the phone.

"It's me." I recognized his voice.

"Hi."

"How are you? You left so fast the other night."

TORN BIBLE

"I'm fine," I answered without responding to his comment.

"Look, I've been meaning to ask you. How's your son doing? How old is he now?"

"Excuse me? Why are you asking about my son?"

"No disrespect. I coach little league and thought maybe he would like to play."

I listened to him go on about his job at CTA and coaching little league. After a few minutes, I lit into him.

"Look, I guess the rundown of your resume and your interest in the kiddies worked for you with those dummies and desperate women you hang out with. I don't give a damn what you do for a living, what you own, or how good you are with the kids. My son is none of your business. I'm not looking for a Baby Daddy. He has one. So save your little tired game and lose my number." I slammed the phone down and mumbled to myself, "That idiot didn't listen when I said I didn't want to talk."

Whatever man I was introduced to and/or went out with or slept with, I treated like the bottom of my shoe. When I looked at them I saw my abusers. When I talked to them, I was talking to my abusers. The voice that was silenced when I was ten, found its way back with a vengeance. I used it to attack their manhood. I used it to tell them they were only good for one thing, just like I was told I was only good for one thing. I was turning the tables.

But I struggled in the silence of the night. I struggled with who I was and who I was becoming. My heart ached. In the depths of my soul I wanted to be the Sharon I was before I found out how I was conceived, about my birth, before the dead man, before the molestation, before the rape, before the marriage, before religion. I wasn't that Sharon anymore. I was someone else, someone I didn't want to be. I didn't know who I was supposed to be.

I knew I was becoming more and more unhinged. I was looking at stuff I shouldn't have been looking at and listening to stuff I shouldn't have been listening to. I was thinking stuff I shouldn't have been thinking and becoming someone no one recognized, including me. I was somewhere I didn't want to be, but too afraid to go where I needed to be.

Men were unsafe. Church was unsafe. God was, other than real, I wasn't sure what God was to me. I wasn't sure what I meant to Him either. I was too afraid to talk to Him again.

I didn't want on me whatever it was that attracted abusers to me. I didn't want the intrusive thoughts that disrupted life so, I fought men. I fought them before they could fight me. I attacked them before they could attack me. I didn't want on me whatever it was the molester, the rapist, my ex-husband or the other men deposited. I didn't want the vulgarity, the perversion, the lust, the anger, the manipulation, or the frustration. I told my therapist the next time I saw her.

CHAPTER **16**

I heard Him!

I TOLD KASEY about my illicit exploits months later. She listened to me talk about the man with no name. She listened to me talk about how I treated men. She listened to me rattle on about this man and that man and… I paused.

She asked, "So, does all of this make you feel any better? Did treating them mean give you any satisfaction?"

I dropped my head and whispered, "No."

"Sharon, what is it you want? Do you even know what you want?"

We sat quietly. She waited for her questions to marinate. She waited for me to think it through.

"I want… I want God to forgive me. I want Him to love me. I want Him to like me again. Do you think He's angry with me? Do you think I have demons? The church people who knew about the mental illness said I had demons. Is that true?"

The compassion in her face was welcoming. "Did you talk to God about how you feel?"

"No. I thought my feelings didn't matter. I thought I couldn't trust my feelings. That's what the church said. You know the faith vs. feelings thing. Besides, I'm too ashamed. Do you really think He wants to hear from me?"

"Of course He does. You're trying to do the right thing by yourself and without trusting God to help you. I believe you want to be right. As far as you having demons, you don't. You care about what God thinks about you too much. What I've noticed about you throughout your therapy with me is your healthy obsession with Jesus."

I looked up at her. "Healthy obsession?"

"Yes. You talk about Him a lot. You haven't noticed?"

"No. Not really."

"You care a lot about your relationship with Him. You care about what He thinks. Even in your anger and acting out, you're aware of Him. You said you wanted Him to forgive you, right?

"Yes."

"You want to ask Him to forgive you now?"

"Um… Yes."

I talked with God for the first time in a long time in Kasey's office. I confessed to Him about how I'd been behaving, about how I treated men and about yelling at Him. I asked Him to forgive me for all of my sins I had committed against Him. I renounced everything that I'd opened myself up to. I renounced everything my encounters, wanted and unwanted had attached to me. I cried uncontrollably. I buried my head in my hands and cried. I was Godly sorry.

Kasey leaned in and took my hands from my face and placed one in her hand while handing me Kleenex to dry my eyes with the other. She waited until I was finished before taking my other hand. My head was still lowered and my eyes closed. I'm not sure why. I just couldn't open them. I didn't know what I was expecting to see, but whatever it was, I wasn't ready to see.

I heard her pray. She thanked God for tugging on my heart and not letting me go too far out of His reach. She thanked Him for hearing my heart's prayer. Tears were still finding their way out of closed eyes. The more she prayed, the more my heart did a little dance of its own. She prayed for my feelings and asked God to let me know they mattered. And then, I heard it. I opened my eyes to see if Kasey noticed anything, heard anything. How could she? The voice or feeling or impression or… was coming from inside of me.

"Trust Me with your feelings."

That's what I heard and felt. I was overcome with emotion.

"Trust Me."

There it was again. Kasey said amen and I didn't notice. I was distracted by what I was hearing, feeling. "Trust Me. Trust Me with your feelings."

I told Kasey what happened. "I heard something."

"What did you hear?"

"I heard, 'Trust Me with your feelings.' Then I heard, 'Just trust Me.'"

She smiled. "Have you ever heard God speak to you?"

"I thought I did. But, this is different."

"It's personal?"

I wiped my eyes with Kleenex again and shook my head up and down, yes.

In all my years of being a believer and going to church, I never felt so personal of a connection with God than in that moment. He actually said something to me, to me and it was about something I'd heard was unimportant for so long, my feelings. He wanted me to trust Him with my feelings. He wanted me to trust Him. I wanted to trust Him, but I was still angry with Him. I still didn't understand why He made Justin leave me. I didn't understand why He let all of those abuses happen to me.

Kasey interrupted my thoughts. "I want you to think about going back to church. Not necessarily the church you came from, but a church or faith community you'll be safe with."

"How will I know which church or faith community is safe for me?"

She smiled again. "Start with trusting God with your feelings, your emotions, and your lack of faith. Tell Him how you feel about church. Tell Him how you feel about everything, even the things you distrust Him about.

"Like Justin?"

"Yes, like Justin. Do you want to talk about him?"

I squirmed.

"Well, start journaling again. Write down how you feel about Justin.

Write about how much you miss him. Ask God about him. Just talk to Him and allow Him to lead you. You'll know. Well, time's up for now. I want you to understand something before I let you go. God never wanted you to ignore your feelings, emotions or your sensitivity. He just doesn't want you to be governed by them. That's why He wants you to give all of that to Him and trust Him. You're well on your way.

The days that followed my visit with Dr. Kasey were emotionally taxing, probably to my own detriment. I took her advice and started journaling again. I also thought about church. In some ways, I overthought church. I wasn't ready to commit, but I knew I needed to go somewhere. I needed to go somewhere to take my deliverance a step further. I was relieved that I could talk to God again. I wrote prayers to Him again. Prayers like:

Lord, it's me Sharon. Thank You for allowing me to talk with You again. Thank You for giving me time to repent. I'm grateful I was able to hear You and I know You want me to trust You with my feelings, trust You with everything. I admit I'm trying. I need help. There are so many things I don't understand, like, why was I born? Why the suicide attempts didn't work? Why so many bad things happened to me? Why I couldn't stay with Justin? If You care so much for me, why did You let all of that happen? I'm sure You know what I'm talking about. Why? Anyway, like I said, Lord, I'm going to keep trying. Amen.

Lord, it's me again. I know I need to go to church, but I'm scared. I don't know where to go and I prefer to go where no one knows me. Also, I have a lot of issues, so, can it be somewhere that has enough power? Can you please make it a safe place for me? I want to feel like I have help, hope, and something to work toward when I leave. Thanks, Amen.

I couldn't say much of anything else, but with that much, I was starting to feel better about God. I was starting to believe that just like I heard Him in Kasey's office, He heard me, even if it was written on paper.

I was listening to gospel music again. I'd stopped listening, when I stopped everything else. I slowly started turning on the radio or searching the internet for music that spoke to where I was. I listened to Walter Hawkins's, "Is There Any Way That I Can Make It." I'd sung it in my teen years in the choir, but this time when I listened, it meant something else, something more. It said what I couldn't say.

I listened to worship songs like, Michael W. Smith's, Here I Am To Worship. I looked at Christian television searching for something that grabbed my spirit. I was looking for something, someone who had enough love and power to help me. I still wasn't trusting people enough to talk or ask for advice about where I should go. I waited on God to lead me. I wasn't sure how that would happen, but I looked for Him to lead anyway.

Jesus Is The Rock church was tucked away in a small, suburban town. If you weren't looking for it or you were driving too fast, you could easily miss it. I watched prayer services on television for weeks. One Sunday morning, instead of relaxing in bed, I jumped up like I was stuck with a needle. I had a burst of energy I hadn't had in a long time. I pulled clothes from the closet, got myself ready before going into my son's room to get him up and ready.

I drove to the church not knowing the exact address. I arrived just before 11:00. I took Jeremy by the hand and hurriedly walked into the vestibule. We were greeted by an older woman with a big smile, no makeup, no jewelry, and a long black skirt and white blouse.

"Hello. Welcome."

TORN BIBLE

I nervously spoke, gave a half smile, looking around the sanctuary for a place to sit.

Knowing I was a visitor, she gave a reassuring smile and said, "Feel free to sit on any side of the church." "Thank you."

The pastor spoke about prayer and deliverance. She talked about how much God loves His people and how much He longs for his people to be free. She said, "He who the Son sets free is free indeed."

When she invited people who needed prayer to come to the altar, I briefly reverted back to the last time I went up to an altar. I remembered the minister who walked away and I froze. I wanted to go, but I was afraid. I was afraid I would be rejected again.

A few people walked up. She said it again. "The altar is open for anyone who needs prayer. We are intercessors and we're here to stand in the gap for you."

I looked up at the pulpit and caught her eyes roaming the room and locking in on me. I looked down at my son who was playing with a toy, took him by the hand and walked up to the front. The pastor smiled at me and looked over at one of her sisters. The sister took me by the hand, while another woman gently took my son's hand from mine.

"I'll just sit here with him. He'll be fine."

I looked down at him, relieved he was still occupied with his little toy truck.

I kept my eye on him while the sister led me to two chairs just across from the woman and my son.

"He's okay," she assured.

I sat in one chair and she sat in the other chair next to me. She put her arm around my shoulder and prayed. She didn't ask me what my prayer request was. She didn't ask who I was and was I saved. She just prayed. I'd never heard anyone pray for me the way she prayed. She didn't sweat. She didn't speak in a million tongues. She didn't make me feel like a project. She just prayed.

Her prayer changed my life. God showed me with her prayer that He heard me. He heard me when I asked Him to lead me somewhere no one knew me. He heard me when I asked him to lead me somewhere that had power to help me. He heard me when I asked him to lead me somewhere I could find hope. I erupted into tears at the thought of knowing He heard me and He answered me. I cried because the sister prayed about everything I was dealing with without having to ask me anything. God told her what to pray about and she heard Him.

CHAPTER 17

The Battle for the Mind

FOR PEOPLE LIKE me who live with depression, "the battlefield of the mind" takes on a whole new meaning. Renewing the mind is a daily, sometimes, minute by minute fight. It takes another level of faith in Jesus to get through and end the day successfully. 2 Timothy 1:7 and Philippians 4:6-8 have been part of my daily devotional for as long as I can remember. Does it help? Emphatically, yes! I know I wouldn't have made it this far without Jesus and the application of scripture.

Denial doesn't equal deliverance. Saying I don't struggle with mental illness when I do is lying, not having faith. Faith in Jesus for my deliverance started with me being honest with myself and Him about where I was and what I was struggling with. My thought and emotional life is my thorn. It's what keeps me dependent on Him. It's what keeps me on my knees. It's what keeps offenses from the religious community out of my heart.

It consistently takes prayer and faith to know Jesus has me in His hands to overcome offense from religious communities. It helps to think maybe it's ignorance and not cruelty that drives misunderstandings about mental illness. I'd like to think most people don't consider how much people with depressive challenges struggle on the inside. It's easy for people to look at others through the lens of their own lives. "Why can't you get up and out of the house? Why is she so bothered by that? How long is she going to keep acting like that?" These are just some of the questions people ask about others who may have mental and emotional struggles.

Depression is an isolated condition. It leaves me feeling alone even when I'm in a room filled with people. It takes away energy to do the simplest things. It affects how I see the world sometimes. It leaves me feeling paralyzed, stuck on the couch or in my bed. In my mind, I'm telling myself, "I need to clean the house. I need to get up and work. I need to go and exercise. I should go out to the mall or to a store. I need to do something." But, there've been many times when my mind ran that list of things I needed to do and I stayed stuck.

Sometimes thoughts race through my mind like sprinters on a track, one idea after another. I find myself race talking just like my thoughts, going from one subject to another. I have to be intentional about slowing myself down. I'm intentional about knowing my triggers, knowing when and how it happens, knowing when I'm anxious or overly tired.

Religious communities are quick to assume someone lacks faith or doesn't want to be free when they don't see immediate changes in a person's life. The most disheartening thing for me was hearing, "You don't want to be well." What people fail to realize is it's possible to be tired and worn out at the thought of trying to move. It's easy for people to see cancer and heart disease as serious life threatening illnesses, but not to see mental illness the same way.

Illnesses of the mind and emotions take a toll on the person who suffers from them. It's a drag to feel and be "heavy" when you don't want to be. It sucks to feel down when you have no reason to be. It's hard to be unhappy when you have every reason to celebrate. It's frustrating to hear, "just think differently," especially when you genuinely try and it doesn't work.

Miracles come in all forms. Miracles can be big or small. For me, a miracle is getting up every day. It's being able to reach out and give hugs when it's awkward. It's walking into a social gathering when I'd prefer to be with just a few friends, family or at home. It's moving past apprehension to talk with strangers on an elevator. My miracle is me.

It takes a special person to be friends with people who have depressive conditions. It takes knowing when to push, when to pull in close, when to give a good swift kick in the pants, if I need it. That person needs patience and possibly a gift of discerning of spirits. For a person who suffers with depressive conditions, it takes prayer and the leading of God to send you the right circle of friends. It took years for me to get the right circle of friends around me. Just like people have faith in God for their physical healing, it takes that kind of faith for mental and emotional healing.

Depression and mental illness can be spiritual as well. There is such a thing as a spirit of fear and a spirit of heaviness. My deliverance from oppression came through surrounding myself with powerful prayer warriors who loved me enough to be truthful and supportive. My responsibility is maintaining my deliverance through therapy when needed, putting on the garment of praise and consistently receiving God's perfect love in place of fear. It means consistent study of the Word of God. It means having sister friends and family who love me and hold me accountable. It means loving and not being too hard on myself. My deliverance is a deliberate process.

My deliverance means saying no without fear of loss. I believe my "no" means something. No is powerful for me because "no" frees me from doing things I don't want to do without fear. For many years, my "no" fell on deaf ears. I said no to the molester. I said no to the rapist. My "no" was ignored. Now, my "no" isn't going to fall on deaf ears again. Now I can say it with confidence. NO!

No, I don't want to go where I'm not comfortable. No, I don't want to be around people I'm not comfortable with. No, I don't feel like talking right now. No, I don't want to go anywhere, right now. No, I don't want to stay in church all day anymore. No, I will not subject myself to abusive church leaders anymore. No, I will not allow anyone else in authority to yell at me or put their hands on me again. No, I don't have to tolerate church abuse to prove my faithfulness to God. No, I don't have to do anything I don't want to do. No!

My peace of mind depends on me guarding my heart and mind from toxic people. My peace and deliverance depends on me trusting God for discerning of spirits to see the motives of people and leaders who may not be good for me. It depends on me discerning who is good for me and not push them away. My peace is dependent upon what I allow myself to think about. It depends on continually casting down imaginations and everything that exalts itself against the knowledge of God, (2 Corinthians 10:5). It's my responsibility to have God's knowledge. It's a process.

CHAPTER **18**

Family Reunion

THE DAY OF my divorce, Gina and I showed up to court early. She'd finally gotten over the fact that I hadn't told her sooner about my problems. Rightly so, she was angry, hurt and disappointed not only about the failed marriage, but more importantly that I'd suffered through abuse and mental illness alone.

She said, "You were alone."

What she meant was, the people I thought I had in my corner, really didn't have my best interest at heart. Maybe they meant well, like so many Christian married women whose husbands didn't treat them right, but fell for the old "Submit to your husband, regardless" sermon. The truth is, my big sister was right, I was truly alone.

I regretfully listened to my husband tell me my single mom, sister, and aunties didn't understand my position as a married woman. The subtleness of luring me from my support system was temporarily successful. I foolishly kept my strong family unit out of my married life because, "I was seeing them too much, we have other things to do or we just don't have time for that." I was seeing less of my family and more and more of his family. Being the type of people who didn't pry into other people's business, no one in my family asked many question apart from, "How are you and do you need anything?"

Each time I'd respond, "No, I'm not okay and I do need all of you," but only in my head. I just couldn't say it out loud because I didn't want Mama to go into a worrying frenzy. Telling my sister while I was in the thick of it would surely have caused her to catch a case. We didn't need jail bars standing in the way of our relationship. My aunties, Marie and Edna, would catch the first Amtrak train or Greyhound bus from Louisiana to Chicago so they could knock some sense into me and drag me back off to Louisiana with them to have my head examined.

My sister was with me. She sat with me until the judge called us up. She sat and waited with me. She knew what divorce was like because she'd been divorced. Her husband who I didn't like turned out to be the jerk I thought he was. She came home too early from work one day and almost killed him. Mama saved her from going to jail. I knew he was a jerk. I saw it. I wish I would have had the same foresight to see who I was marrying too. I didn't see it. Oh, wait. I did see it. I just didn't trust it or understand what I knew and what I saw. So, here we were.

When I walked back into my house, I sat on the sofa and breathed. I breathed deeply, in and out. It was the beginning of exhaling pain, fear, and anger, and inhaling peace, joy and love that would take years to completion. I'd gotten out of one battle and into another. It would be the beginning of the bewilderment of divorce. Not just my divorce, but my son's divorce too. It was the start of missed weekend visits, late child care pickups or not at all, missed financial support payments and no support at all. It was more anxiety and frustration of not wanting to be the only parent for my son. It was the realization that at least one parent got to choose while the other one didn't.

TORN BIBLE

Just prior to filing for divorce, I visited with my Auntie Sally, Mama's oldest sister, who'd moved to Chicago from New Orleans for a few years. She lived in a two flat brownstone in the heart of the west side. It was summertime in Chicago. The corner of Monroe Street smelled of a mixture of barbeque, fried chicken and weed. The sidewalks were covered with scattered paper, soda pop cans, beer bottles and restaurant bags from the shenanigans of previous nights. Porches were filled with people talking loud and hanging out. Car speakers were heard two blocks away and kids played and ran through water from fire hydrants.

Upstairs on the 2nd floor is where I exhaled. Auntie Sally was sitting on the side of her bed when I walked into her room. I leaned down to give her a hug and in her embrace I felt the strength of Grandma. How I missed her and wished she was still here with me. I missed our conversations we had over a bowl of cornbread and butter milk. I missed the way she smacked when she ate. But, in that moment, I knew she was with me. Auntie Sally's big chocolate arms embraced me like a warm blanket on a cold winter's night. For a few seconds, when I closed my eyes, I could see Grandma's smooth round face with her soft cheeks formed into a slight smile. I used to love pressing my face against hers so my small face sunk into her jaws. I wanted to tell Grandma about everything. I wanted to sit with her over that bowl of cornbread and butter milk and spill my guts. Auntie Sally held on tightly to me as tears gushed out of my eyes. In her New Orleans twang accent, she said. "Chile, sit down here on this bed and talk to me."

In a matter of minutes, I told her my married life's story. I told her how I'd lost myself, how I was trying to be a good Godly wife, but couldn't do it any longer. I told her I didn't know how to trust my own judgement anymore. I told her how afraid I was and how I wanted all of the pain to go away. She listened and occasionally nodded. I shared with her the things I'd endured and how it nearly destroyed me.

Mid– sentence, Auntie Sally stopped me. In her scolding voice she lovingly said, "Now we don't tolerate that kind of behavior from no man. You just remember you're stronger than that. You don't ever have to stay in that kind of situation. You hear me?"

"Yes ma'am. I hear you. So, I'm doing the right thing?" I asked, seeking more affirmation. Although I'd gotten approval from my pastor, hearing her say it too gave me comfort.

"Yes indeed," she said.

All three of my aunties had been married and divorced. Each one of them had experienced abuse and/or cheating of some kind and chose not to be that kind of woman, the kind of woman who stayed and made excuses for her husband, the kind of woman who blamed herself. More importantly, each one had failed to find the man who would be most like Granddaddy.

Mama had her experiences of controlling and stalking men too, one being Deacon Jackson. But, like Granddaddy prophesied, Mama wasn't taking nothing off nobody, especially no man. She didn't mind picking up a cast iron skillet or a knife to defend herself or one of her sisters from a man who liked fighting women.

It was during those talks with Mama and Auntie Sally that I gained strength. Mama and her sisters were different than most women from their generation. They fought back. They respected themselves and demanded respect from others, including men. Like most people, they made their mistakes, but they didn't waddle in them.

Mama always said, "Two wrongs don't make a right."

She made the mistake of trusting Deacon Jackson and found herself in an affair. She recovered by quickly breaking it off with him and making better choices going forward, despite his constant stalking. Instead of aborting me, she kept me. She raised me the best way she knew how. She went on to live a life of holiness, real holiness, the kind of holiness that had nothing to do with clothes. It's the kind of holiness that commanded the respect of other women.

Divorcing my husband meant reuniting with my family. It meant gaining strength from a legacy of strong, hardworking women. I would later learn that legacy of strength went way back to Grandma, Great Grandma, and my great aunties. It meant the beginning of discovering me. I realized how blessed I was to have a family who didn't mind fighting for the people they loved.

I reconnected with cousins I hadn't talked with in years. I started going back to family reunions every year. I traveled more. I laughed more. I started surrounding myself with my sister friends' families who quickly became my families as well. I started benefiting from folks who embraced my son and me as if we'd been in their lives forever.

I talked more to my uncles, especially my favorite uncle who I affectionately call my "Uncle Daddy." I couldn't really pin point what it was that connected my heart to him. Maybe it was his calm demeanor. Maybe it was his intellect. Maybe it was in the way he cared for my aunt and cousins. Maybe it was his educational ambitions. Maybe it was his strong faith in God. Maybe it was his ability to remain steady in turbulent times. Maybe it's in the way he says what he means and means what he says without the need to raise his voice or his hand. Maybe it's because his personality reminds me of Granddaddy. Maybe it's all of it.

Uncle Daddy is who I call when I need a dad to talk to. He's who I call when I need advice. I call him when I want to share successes and failures. I call him when I need to hear a calming male voice. I call him just to tell him I love him. When I look at him, I see a man who's clearly after God's heart.

Part 4
Better Is the End

CHAPTER **19**

Changing Direction

I WAS NEVER invited to his home. I didn't know his address. He called to ask me to come over to his home for a talk as if I'd been a legitimate daughter routinely going to check on her father. I was in my early 40s and he was in his late 80s. He'd spent the last five years prior to the phone call trying to make up for thirty five plus years of rejection, denial, abandonment, and scandal.

He was much older, sickly, and his fading mortality was staring him in the face. He was anxious for me to know his family. He was suddenly inviting me to reunions and family gatherings. He'd plead with me every time we talked, as if he was reading from a script. "I want everyone to know who you are. You're my daughter. You're not a mistake."

He was trying to convince himself more than me. I'd already grieved the father/daughter relationship I never had. I'd already grieved the family who never really accepted me.

I'd eulogized and buried my dreams of one day being fully embraced as a Jackson at his birthday dinner. I got an invitation to his 85th surprise birthday celebration. One of his daughters even asked Mama if I'd received their invitation to "Daddy's" birthday celebration in the mail.

Mama came home from church, happy to relay the message from her. "Your sister wanted to know if you got your invitation to your dad's birthday celebration." She eagerly waited for my response.

I asked, "Who?"

Her smile faded. "Sharon, don't be like that."

I ignored her and asked again, "From whom, for whom?"

She answered knowing she wasn't going to win this one.

"I told her I got it."

"You're going, right?"

"I'm not sure yet."

"Don't you think it's time to let your guard down?"

"How was church, Ma?" I asked, changing the subject. I wasn't interested in feeling the same emotions I felt when I was a child, emotions I didn't have words for.

I decided the day before to go to the birthday celebration. I wasn't sure why. Maybe I was hoping by some miracle things would be different. Maybe I was hoping he wasn't lying again when he said he wanted me to be his daughter. Maybe I was just trying to please Mama.

Mama, my niece and I drove over 30 miles to the west side from the south suburbs of Chicago. The invitation gave me a sense of confidence and acceptance. The invitation erased feelings of insecurity and anxiety until I walked into the banquet hall and took a seat at one of the round tables.

Deacon Jackson hadn't made his arrival yet. All of his family was there, some who didn't know I existed while some clearly knew I existed. I looked around the neatly decorated room, observing stares of disbelief from nieces and nephews who'd obviously been privy to me being their family's secret.

I watched them whisper to one another. The conspicuous group of young people looked at each other, over to me, and back at each other. My eyes roamed around the room to different tables that were filling up with people. Some people were talking among themselves. Others were whispering among themselves while their heads turned slightly toward my table. I felt as if I'd walked into a den of lions waiting to champ at me.

My niece, British, gasped. "Auntie, we should leave. They bogus for this! This ain't funny."

I turned to see what had her so upset all of a sudden. Was she looking around the room too? Did she notice people whispering too? I saw her looking down at the evening program that featured Deacon Jackson's picture. She opened it and, turned it to the back and the front again.

"What are you looking at?"

"Auntie did you see this?"

"See what?"

Mama knew what was going on and tried hard to gain control of the commotion at our table. "British, be quiet. You're too loud."

"Granny, this isn't right."

I looked at my program that I'd first ignored, trying to find the reason for her outburst. She pointed her finger to the list of children fathered by Deacon Jackson.

"Auntie, they had the nerve to invite you here and didn't even bother to put your name down."

She was right. I looked at the list of names and saw natural children, step children, and God children. I saw everyone's name except my own.

I held my head down longer, staring at the page trying hard not to let the tears that were welling up in my eyes fall down my cheeks. I kept my head down until I was able to look up without my emotions on my face. It took me a few minutes. Mama didn't ask questions. She waited until I could regroup. She waited until I decided what to do next. She waited and prayed. She didn't say she prayed. I knew she waited and prayed.

When I finally looked up from my program that didn't include my name, I looked right into the eyes of one of his daughters. She was standing against the wall looking at me like she was watching a sad movie with me as the leading character. I wondered did she plan it that way. Did she position herself in front of me to see how much pain I'd be in? How else could she happen to be in that spot at that time?

Her eyes told the story of her heart. Her eyes said, "I know you exist, but I never wanted you to. I don't want to have to explain you to my daddy's friends. I don't want other people who may not know you exist to know now. I know you're hurt. I don't care. I never cared. I want to keep my father's secret from his friends. No one can know about you." I saw her heart in her eyes. I saw that it was cold.

Deacon Jackson still hadn't arrived. Senior citizens were catching up, introducing grandkids and great grand kids to one another. I stood up from the table, gathered my things and headed for the door. British was on my heels, huffing and puffing as if she was on her way to a gang fight. I didn't feel like fighting. I didn't feel like anything. I was void of energy. Mama slowly, reluctantly followed. She wasn't ready to leave. She had friends there. She had relationships there. She was comfortable there. She was comfortable just like never leaving the church, except this time, no matter how comfortable she was, she left an uncomfortable place for me.

Jamie, one of Deacon Jackson's grandchildren stepped in front of me. "Sharon, don't leave. You know who you are."

Blank stare. No words. I politely moved past her and out the door. Once inside my car, I screamed. I just screamed. I let out a full cry with a waterfall of tears. I felt a mixture of anger, hurt, betrayal and deceit. Which sister invited me? Whose idea was this? Did they invite me just to humiliate me?

I was stuck, stuck in the driver's seat, stuck staring at the steering wheel. Mama and British hopped in the passenger side and back seat respectably. "Auntie, you okay?"

I sighed and shook my head, no. I had nothing to say and apparently neither did Mama. I put the car in reverse and backed out of the driveway. I put the car in drive and headed 30 miles back south.

This time I didn't stop the tears that welled up in my eyes. I let them freely fall down my face. I was in the driver's seat and decided in that moment that it would be my choice which direction I was willing to go. My destination was up to me. I chose not to expect to be part of a family who didn't want me. I let my dreams of having a real father die. I let my dreams of having brothers and more sisters die.

I cried all the way home. I cried out my expectations. I cried out my desires for a relationship with Deacon Jackson. The tiny crack in my heart I kept open in hopes of my dad one day being able to fill, finally closed. I cried it closed. I buried it, never to be resurrected again. Whatever I expected, whatever dreams I had for more siblings, were gone. I couldn't afford to keep expecting and dreaming about any of it.

CHAPTER **20**

Revelations

DEACON JACKSON CONFESSED to me the reason he'd rejected me all those years ago. We sat on the porch of his house and watched as shirtless men and women with multicolored hair walked up and down the block with a beer in one hand and a lit cigarette in the other. It was the third time in a year I'd been invited to his house to talk. The first time I went, I paused at the door before ringing the bell. I pondered whether to quickly walk back to my car, drive off and tell him something had come up. I looked around me before I mustered up the nerve to ring the bell. His wife answered.

"Hi. How are you? Come on in."

I was frozen. I couldn't move. It was the first time in over 40 years she was genuinely friendly towards me. In the past, she tolerated me whenever she saw me. She said it again.

"Come on in."

I walked slowly behind her into the living room where Deacon Jackson was sitting. We had the familiar awkward conversation while I nervously shifted on the chair, forward, then backward, right side, then left side.

REVELATIONS

This time, sitting on his front porch, he sat staring at the different ones walking around and occasionally blinked his eyes. I waited for him to start talking.

He said, "Your mother wouldn't marry me, so I married someone else."

Right out of the blue, that's what came out of his mouth. He didn't know Mama had already told me why she wouldn't marry him after his first wife died. She said she knew he hadn't changed and it would probably be another woman who'd end up in the same situation she found herself in all those years ago.

I asked, "Weren't you already married? What did my mother not marrying you have to do with you rejecting me?" Knowing full well his answer, I asked anyway.

"By the time I asked, my wife had passed away. Like I said, your mother said no."

Whether what he said was true or not, I'm not sure. He'd lied to me more times than I could count. What I knew to be true was his rejection of me. What I knew to be true was I wasn't allowed to contact him during my childhood or teen years. I was more inclined to believe Mama.

"I was rejected by your children my entire life. Do you remember when I called your house when I was 12 years old and you told me to never call your house again?"

He sighed. "I'm so sorry I did that. I allowed too much to go on back then."

I asked him the one question I've always wanted to ask. I turned my folding chair around to face him and asked.

123

TORN BIBLE

"Why do your kids hate me?"

He didn't dispute it. Instead, he went on to explain.

"Well, when you were a baby, I didn't acknowledge you at first, but when your mother started bringing you to church, I was carrying you around and holding you all the time. My kids were even taking a liking to you. But my new wife, well, she knew what happened, about you and how all of that came about. She told the kids if they accepted you as their sister, it would be a disgrace to their mother's memory." I was stunned. Nothing could've prepared me for that explanation. I didn't know how to respond.

The stories I heard were true. The guilt I was feeling about their mother dying because I was born rang true in his confirmation of their hatred for me. They didn't want to bring disgrace to their mother's memory. The fact they were much older and could think for themselves when I was a baby apparently didn't change anything. But it didn't explain why they liked and talked with Mama. Maybe it was because she was still at the church and a church mother who everyone respected.

He continued. "I should've put a stop to it when she told them that." He paused and looked up to the sky, perhaps hoping God would help him with more words to say. "I want to apologize to you for all of it. You're not a mistake. You are meant to be here."

"I know that," I answered.

After years of trying to eliminate myself from the world, it felt good to finally know I was meant to keep breathing. I was breathing even though I hadn't quite figured out how to live.

When I met up with Mama, I asked her about what Deacon Jackson said.

"Well, that could be true. I wouldn't take all of what he says to heart. Always remember, there are two sides to every story."

I pushed back. "They were old enough to know right from wrong. If they listened to the step mother, which I think they did, it's on them. I can believe him this time because of how they've treated me over the years."

Mama didn't say anything.

"You know what, Mama?" I paused. "That's okay. Never mind."

I walked away from her. I started to bring up the issue of her relationship with the siblings, including my brother who was now her pastor again. I opted against it. It never went well and I always walked away feeling unheard.

CHAPTER **21**

Confronting Resentment

I RESENT HER. That's what I confessed to myself before I confessed it to God. I was upset with myself for feeling resentment toward my own mother. I didn't want to, but I did. I asked God if I could love someone so much and still resent them. I loved Mama so much I couldn't bear to think that I felt anything other than love for her. I was stuck. I didn't understand the why behind her decisions and I resented her because of them.

Why did she stay at the church? Why didn't she go to another church? Why was she so friendly with the siblings? Why did they talk to her, but not me? Why didn't she know how it made me feel? Why did she want me to ignore my own feelings about them and the situation? Did she want me to overlook everything? Why didn't she want to talk about it?

I could never understand how Mama could have relationships with siblings who didn't have relationships with me. How she could hold long phone conversations with them, be her pastor's (my brother's) confidant and intercessor? How could she have so much respect for people who didn't talk to me? It wasn't enough to send messages from church. "Tell Sharon this. Tell Sharon that." Second hand messages weren't relationships even if it was Mama delivering the messages. It hurt. It really hurt. Getting her to see and hear that hurt was a daunting task.

I understood where she was coming from. I understood her heart. Mama is a fighter. She never runs away from her problems. She's a reconciler. She's a prayer warrior. She forgives and forgets. She's from that generation that ignored whatever stinks, overlooked elephants in the room, and kept walking, stepping over comatose issues, hoping they'd miraculously die off and bury themselves.

She wanted me to be like her. She wanted me to be happy they sent messages home from church. She wanted me to forgive and forget. She wanted me to be the bigger person, be the prayer warrior, and be the loving sister. She wanted me to keep knocking on doors that were never going to open for me. She wanted me to keep visiting a church that was a horrible nightmare. She wanted me to speak to her pastor who treated me like a visitor instead of his sister whenever I came to the church to drop her off or pick her up.

I asked God for the right time and the right way to say what I needed to say to Mama. I asked God to help her see my pain and hear my heart on the matter. My faith in God evolved with each new day, one issue at a time. I was learning to trust Him to remove the invisible barrier between me and Mama. I needed to address the church-sibling issue that refused to die.

My time had come. It was time to start a war to get to peace. Mama came home and tried to deliver her usual messages from one or more of the siblings.

"Mama, please don't give me anymore messages from them."

The look on her face said, if you weren't an adult, I'd slap you dead in your mouth.

TORN BIBLE

She stood frozen in one spot in disbelief. She couldn't believe I didn't say my usual, "Okay."

"What did you say?" She did not mean it as a question.

She sat down on the living room sofa still dressed in her white Mother's Board dress and hat. It was 1st Sunday. I sat on the love seat across from her.

"Mama, no disrespect, but, I would like it if you'd stop bringing home messages from them. If they wanted to have a relationship with me and talk with me, they know where they can find me."

"Sharon, I wish you would just stop being so difficult. You're not the easiest person to talk to, you know." That would usually be my cue to leave the room. This time I stayed.

"Why do you think it's hard to talk to me?" I asked.

"You're just so standoffish and funny acting."

"I thought you understood me?"

"I do. I just want you to try a little harder to be friendly."

"You don't think I'm friendly?"

"You could stand to be a little more outgoing."

I paused and sighed.

"Well, I'm not outgoing. I'm extremely introverted and withdrawn. But, you know that already."

She didn't say anything.

And then it came to me, appealing to her sense of family.

"Ma, you and your siblings are really close. As a matter fact, you're pretty close to our whole family, right? Well, can you imagine seeing them every Sunday or every time you went to church and not being able to talk with them or have a relationship with them?"

She sat quietly, but exhaled. "No."

"Right, you can't imagine that because it's never happened to you and it never will. Just think about our family and how you'd feel if you didn't have a relationship with any of them, even if you saw them all the time."

"I can't imagine," she answered.

"That's what I've been going through all of these years. I've had to go to the same church and endure the pain of having a family I'll never be part of. To get messages from them through you only digs the knife deeper into my heart. Even though I'm not at that church anymore, I can't heal because you keep pulling the scab off. I want you to hear my heart. I want you to see how much it hurts."

She listened. This time she listened, finally heard me, and apologized. She finally heard the voice I'd lost with her too. I didn't know I'd lost my voice with her until that moment. It happened every time she wanted me to talk to them, when they clearly didn't want to talk to me, and every time she wanted me to treat them like family.

I tried talking. I tried to say how I felt. I tried to express myself. I tried to say no, but she didn't hear me. My no didn't mean anything, just like when I said no to my abusers and they didn't hear me either. This time I had to fight for my no again, and I won.

CHAPTER **22**

Seeing Why God Blocked him

DEACON JACKSON TOLD me each time we talked that he wanted a real relationship with me. But, that twelve year old girl stood up inside me and said no. I couldn't bring myself to open my heart. I was never fully comfortable talking with him. The confession or apology didn't change how I felt. I was completely guarded, waiting for the day he'd say again, "Don't call me."

I started spending more time with him. Deacon Jackson would take me to breakfast, sometimes lunch. He'd talk and I'd listen. In those moments, I began to see God's protection. I saw what God was keeping me from. As much pain as I experienced not knowing him, knowing him would have been catastrophic. I listened as he talked about his children as if he didn't know them or love them. I knew he did in his own way.

I listened to his disappointments for the decisions they made. I listened as he said things only a disappointed parent would say. I found myself defending people I didn't know. I was defending people who had rejected me.

I was saying, "Don't you think you should be a little more understanding? Don't you think you're being unrealistic?" Or, "Haven't you made mistakes before?"

When he would show disdain for my mother being a strong woman, naturally I defended her like a pit bull.

"Your mother wouldn't listen to me. She could've been better off had she just married me, but she had to be at church all the time. She had to work in that kitchen all the time. She just wouldn't listen to me."

In those brief conversations with Deacon Jackson, I saw God was protecting me from a father who didn't value his children properly and, at times, didn't speak well of them away from their presence. Maybe he didn't speak well of them in their presence. I can't say for sure. It made me wonder. I listened as he spewed venom. This is too easy for him. He didn't raise me. He didn't know me. How could it be so easy for him to talk with me about something so personal?

God protected me from being raised by a man who apparently lacked compassion for his children. He protected me from a mother who would've been controlled, battered and unable to raise strong, independent women. He protected me from not having a close knit family. He showed me through these brief encounters that it's not always a good thing to have a dad in the house if he's not properly attentive or just not right.

I also saw in him the type of men I attracted. I saw he didn't have to live with me or have a relationship with me to leave a negative mark on me. Whenever possible, I observed his relationships a little more closely. I observed relationships that weren't very healthy, relationships I wouldn't have been happy with anyway. Spending time with him made me grateful I hadn't done so sooner.

CHAPTER **23**

When Deacon Jackson Died, I Saw the Heart of God

MAMA HANDED ME the phone. "Someone's on the phone for you," she said.

I was sitting at my desk in my room reading when I got the call. It was Mama's pastor, my brother. He talked to me as if we went way back. He talked as if he'd just talked with me last week, when in fact, I couldn't remember the last time, if any, we'd had any type of conversation. Now, here he was on the phone.

"Yeah, hey." he said.

"Hi."

"I was just calling to let you know Dad's not doing too well. We don't think he's going to make it, just in case you wanted to go and see him."

"Okay. Thanks for letting me know."

I handed Mama the phone. She never left my room. She waited for me to say something as she took the phone from my hand. She anticipated bad news.

"He said he wasn't doing well. He said he was calling to tell me just in case I wanted to go to the hospital to see him."

"Are you going to go?"

"I'm not sure."

She left the room, opting not to press. I was in a state of nothingness. I stared at the computer screen that wasn't on and immediately decided not to go. I couldn't think of a good reason to go, just like I couldn't think of reasons to go to other siblings' funerals when they passed away. Not because I didn't have the common concern any human being with a heart had, but because I didn't feel like I belonged. I didn't feel like a daughter or a sister. I didn't feel like family.

I was talking to God more and more and He was talking to me more and more. This time I heard Him again. "Time is running out. You need to go." That's what I heard. "You need to go."

Mama was pleased when I told her. I asked if she would go with me to the hospital. She happily said yes. It was Friday.

Saturday morning we got up and set out on our journey to the western suburbs. On the way, Mama's pastor, my brother, called her. He called to warn that one of his sisters was at the hospital and encouraged Mama to continue on to the hospital and not be distracted by her. Mama told me as much when she got off the phone with him.

"You know who is there."

I nodded, knowing exactly who.

"He said we shouldn't turn around, but continue on."

I nodded yes and kept driving. At that point, it wasn't about her.

No matter how awkward I felt, I wanted desperately to be obedient to God and just go. Mama and I got to his room, walked in and stood near the door. His daughter, my sister, was sitting by his bed holding his hand. He was incoherent. She looked over at us and said, "This isn't a good time." Not hello, but, "it's not a good time." We didn't move. I wasn't leaving. I drove a good 30 miles and I wasn't leaving.

Minutes went by. Finally she stood up and said. "Sharon, you can come over here and sit next to Daddy." I paused, thinking, so now you remember my name. Now you want me to sit near "Daddy." I looked at Mama and she nodded for me to go over and sit. She followed me, standing on the other side of his bed. His daughter moved closer to the wall and called someone. Deacon Jackson was kicking covers off and trying to fight whenever me or Mama attempted to put the covers back.

"Dad, quit fighting and talk to Sharon."

That's what his daughter said. I didn't say anything to her. I stood up and got closer to him. He looked over at me and tried desperately to say something. He struggled to say my name, but I made out the first few syllables. His eyes, which I hadn't noticed before were a grayish color, grew big. He looked at me, pleading. In my spirit I knew what he was trying so hard to say. I saw it in his eyes. I saw it when he reached for me.

"It's okay. You can rest. I forgive you." I said to him. I rubbed his head and said it again.

"It's okay," I assured him, and meant it. "I forgive you."

I could hear the sister on the phone telling whoever she was talking with, "Yeah, his other daughter's here now." I continued to ignore her.

Mama and I stayed a little while longer. She fussed at him to quit fighting and keep the covers on him. I stood by his bed, rubbing his head and looking at him. I saw a very sick, vulnerable old man. In that moment, all the pain I endured over years vanished. None of it mattered anymore. He calmed down a bit. The room grew quiet until the sister asked, "Why don't you put your number in my phone and we can keep in touch." I was caught completely off guard. I honestly wasn't interested, but put my number in her phone anyway, knowing full well that she'd probably delete it when I left. I wasn't holding my breath. I knew she'd never use it. This was the same sister who didn't include me on his birthday program.

Deacon Jackson passed away two or three days later at 92 years old. His funeral was scheduled for the following Saturday at the church where his son was pastor. I was at peace. I obeyed God. I genuinely forgave him and had closure with him. I still needed help getting through the funeral that I often said I'd never attend whenever the time came. Here I was, being nudged to go. I prayed for strength right up until and during his funeral. I solicited the backup, without effort, from my big sister Gina and a few of my sister friends to be there with me.

My son Jeremy and I got to the church just before the wake started. His family hadn't arrived yet. I parked my car at the end of the block and waited for Gina and my sister friends to arrive. I wasn't going in without them. I knew it would be an awkward experience, but no one could've prepared me for how awkward and just how downright sad peoples' behaviors would be. We all walked in together and sat in the back of the church. One of Deacon Jackson's nieces was sitting near me and walked over to give me hug.

"I'm glad you're here," she said.

"Thank you."

After introducing herself to my son, she politely sat a few seats down from me.

"The family is here," the niece said to me.

I tilted my head slightly to the side, misunderstanding her. I wasn't sure why she was telling me. She knew what I was thinking. She knew how I felt. She's always known how things were, but had no voice to make a difference.

"Sharon. Come on. You're family. You deserve to walk in with them just as much as they do."

I looked over at my sisters and they shrugged their shoulders.

One of them said, "It's up to you. Whatever you decide, we got you. We'll be sitting right over here." I looked at Gina who was sitting on the other side of the church. She knew and she gave me an approving look which meant, go ahead, you'll be fine.

Jeremy and I walked into the room where the family was gathering to walk in. His niece and Jeremy never left my side. Both of them knew without saying it that I needed someone to walk with me. Everyone was standing around waiting for instructions. No one said anything to us, not even hello. The pastor, the same brother who called to tell me "Dad" wasn't doing good, looked at me and said nothing. His daughters looked at me and said nothing.

A few other nieces and nephews saw me said, "Hi, Auntie."

"Hi," I responded.

Most of them said nothing and just stared.

Jeremy said, "Ma. These people are weird."

"I know. It'll be over soon and we can leave."

He shrugged.

The pastor gave instructions and led the way into the wake, saying whatever preachers say. We slowly followed behind. Jeremy and I got to the front, bypassed the casket and headed back to our seats in the back of the church. We sat near my sister friends. It was where I felt safe.

The church filled up quickly while the wake went on. Mama was on her post sitting with the Mother's Board. Gina was still on the other side of the church, talking and catching up with old friends. I sat talking with my sister friends while my son occupied himself with his phone. One of the members came to where I was sitting.

"Sharon, I'm going to escort you up to the front to sit with your siblings."

"No, thank you."

"Are you sure?"

"Yes. I'm fine back here."

She gave a confusing look, but obliged. A few minutes later, another lady came over and asked, "Can you please come up and sit with the family?"

"No, thank you." I was starting to feel pressure and irritation. My sister friends kept talking to me, trying to keep me distracted.

The family side was filling up, so my sister friends had to move their seats to the corner. They were clearly still in my view in case I needed to look over at them for reassuring glances. It was a few minutes before the start of the service when one of the pastor's daughters came and sat next to me. "Hi, Auntie," she said rather loudly.

I said, "Hi."

"Why are you sitting back here? You're supposed to be up front with the rest of the family. You're supposed to be on the front row."

I looked around me, after hearing whispering. "That's her?"

"Yeah, that's her. That's his other daughter."

Thanks to "my niece," attention was drawn to me.

She continued. "It don't look right for you to be way back here."

Before that day, I'd never had a conversation with her for more than an hour. Now, she was talking with me as if we had a relationship, when I actually knew nothing much about her. However, she'd always been respectful and kind whenever she saw me. So, I couldn't be angry with her for trying. She continued. "Can't you just go ahead up there?"

I knew her pleading with me to sit on the front row had nothing to do with me, so I thought, but everything to do with optics. As if on cue, the usher was standing nearby waiting. I looked in my sister friends' direction. They were close enough to hear the exchange. I sighed.

WHEN DEACON JACKSON DIED, I SAW THE HEART OF GOD

To avoid a lingering exchange with the niece, Jeremy and I followed the usher to the front. Jeremy whispered, "Why we got to go up here?"

"To avoid drama."

One of the sisters made a space for me to sit next to her and announced, "Oh, your son can sit a few rows back with the other grandkids."

"I looked at Jeremy and put my finger to my lips, motioning him not to say anything.

I knew what he was thinking. The other grandkids? Really?

He shook his head, shrugged and followed the usher a few rows back. My eyes followed to pinpoint his exact location. After knowing where he was sitting, I looked back further to lock eyes with my sister friends. They gave a reassuring nod.

I sat on the front row around people I really didn't know, cousins I'd never met, and siblings I didn't talk to. Service was starting. The pastor was walking back in adorned in his priestly robe with other pastors and ministers following. One of Deacon Jackson's daughters, also a pastor of a church, stopped to hug each family member on the front row. She lovingly hugged the person to the left of me, looked me in my eyes, moved past me, and proceeded to hug the other sister to the right of me. After giving her hugs, she proceeded to the pulpit to sit with the other pastors.

Any other time I would've felt devastated. I probably would have left. This time, I felt a little offended, but more of a righteous indignation. She literally looked me in my face, didn't say hi, didn't hug me, but purposely moved past me, hugged others and walked into a place of sacredness. She sat in a place of ordination. She sat in a place of prayer, prepared to talk to God, but couldn't find it in her heart to talk to me. I was baffled. I sat down and looked over at a friendly face. An evangelist I knew was sitting nearby. She smiled at me and shook her head, from side to side, letting me know she saw what happened. I smiled back at her. God used her as another source of strength for me through occasional smiles and nods each time I looked in her direction.

I would later find out that she was one of the people who were fighting for me when I was a little girl. She knew my story. She knew what happened and she was one of several who always fought for me. The service went on with talks, songs and stories about Deacon Jackson. I heard people share personal memories of times shared with him. I listened to aldermen and state officials who he'd known over the years. I felt like I was sitting in a sea of sharks. I felt darts at my back. I was still hearing whispers from family members who were asking questions. "Who is she?" No doubt, some of them didn't know the Sharon Green listed with Deacon Jackson's other children on the obituary.

I wanted to leave, but instead, I listened to the pastor, "my brother," give the eulogy. I listened as he talked about him and his siblings as children. He talked about how "their dad" worked hard to provide for them. I listened as he talked about how he made sure they had a warm place to stay and food to eat. I listened to stories of family gatherings. I listened to him talk about a man I'd never known that way. I listened as he talked about a man who never provided for me. Just before he started his eulogy, his daughter who didn't speak, prayed a prayer. But not before sharing her memories of waiting up for him to get home from work. She shared memories of special talks and moments. She was clearly a "daddy's girl."

I sat and watched family members cry and mourn the loss of someone they knew and loved. I listened, but I heard another voice. I heard that voice again. I heard the same "voice" I heard in Kasey's office.

"That's how you see Me." That's what God said to me sitting in my "dad's" funeral.

"You sat in church for years listening to other peoples' relationships with Me. You listened to other people talk about how I've provided for them and how I love them. But, you've always been hesitant and saw Me the way you saw him." I was sitting there listening to a whole speech from God to me.

He said, "I'm not him. I didn't abandon you. I've always been here. I'm your Father. You are "Daddy's girl, My girl."

I quickly wiped a tear from my eye before anyone saw and wrongly assumed I was crying about Deacon Jackson. He was still talking.

"You've been working hard to provide for yourself and earn love when I've always been providing for you and loving you. You've been trying to protect yourself when I've always protected you. I'm not him. I'm your real Father and I love you."

There was an overwhelming peace that overtook me. The pastor was at the end of his eulogy and I was done. He called for the funeral directors to prepare for the final viewing. I stood there while people greeted siblings and other family members as they marched around. People I didn't know politely spoke to me and shook my hand. Things were getting a bit too chaotic for me and I'd had enough. I looked back at Jeremy and motioned for him to come follow me. When he made his way to the front, I led him through the middle aisle. I briefly paused to tell Mama I was leaving. This time, the "pastors" spoke. I said, "Hi," and kept walking toward the door. I caught the eye of Gina and my sister friends. They knew I was ready to leave and they made their way through the crowd toward the door where I was waiting.

There was no need to go to the burial. I'd already buried him. I wasn't interested in breaking bread with people I had no relationship with and who still clearly didn't want one with me either. Instead, I spent the rest of the afternoon with my sister friends after I took Jeremy to spend the afternoon with his friends. On the way, Jeremy told me about his experience at the funeral.

"Ma, I almost got into it with a few of those people I was sitting around."

"What? What happened?"

"They made me mad. They were talking about you. A couple of them was asking who you was. They was like, who is Sharon Green? And then one of the girls was like, that's one of granddaddy's daughters. The one girl was like, what?"

"Really, all of that was going on back there?"

"Yeah, that same girl said, "Girl, it's a long story. I'll have to tell you about it later." They were talking like I wasn't sitting there. So I said, "That's my mother."

She said, "I know who yo Mama is."

"Ma, I know I'm not supposed to hit girls, but I wanted to slap that girl. She was so rude, Ma. I mean, she made me mad."

"I'm sure that did make you angry. I'm proud of you though. I'm glad you didn't lose your temper. It wasn't worth it. Don't worry. You'll never have to deal with that again."

I could see out of the corner of my eye he was studying my facial expressions.

"You okay, Ma?"

"Yeah, I'm okay."

"Why did they treat us that way?"

I sighed. I hadn't realized until then I wasn't the only one experiencing this. By default, Jeremy was too. "It's a long story, but it had nothing to do with you. Let's just say, I'm not a real part of the family. I've always been open and honest with you and I'm not going to stop now. Deacon Jackson was more of a sperm donor than a real dad to me." He didn't say anything else. Instead we listened to R & B oldies all the way home.

Later, that afternoon my sister friends picked me up and took me out to lunch. They had more enlightening things to share with me from Deacon Jackson's funeral. While I was feeling like a target up front, they were controlling themselves from attacking the people in the back who were apparently fascinated with me. "Girl, if we weren't there with you, we would have never believed all of this happened."

One of my sisters said, "Yeah."

The other one said, shaking her head, "We were overhearing over grown people back there talking about, "Is that her? Wow. I have never seen her before. That's the other daughter? Yeah, she looks like them." I listened as they shared with me the same experiences I'd had for years.

"Oh, my God," one of my sister friends said. "We thought we were going to have to fight somebody. They were back there having whole conversations about you."

I nodded and I wasn't surprised.

"We never experienced anything like that."

"I'm sure you haven't," I responded. "Ya'll was back there listening to foolishness and Jeremy was listening to foolishness too."

"What? What was he hearing?"

"He was listening to Deacon Jackson's grandchildren ask questions about me. He heard one of them promise to share the juicy details with the others later. It's a mess. It's been over 40 years of mess."
"Wow, I bet you any kind of money what that repast is like."

"Oh, I'm sure." My sister friends and Gina made that day bearable for me. God made it revelatory.

CHAPTER **24**

Layers of Forgiveness

KASEY SAID I had layers of un-forgiveness. She said I had to work through each layer at a time. She told me to list each person who'd harmed me in any way. She warned that it would be difficult and in many ways painful to get through. She stressed the need to push through until I addressed each person and each issue. It would take years to work through it all.

The Ex-Husband

Jesus said in (Matthew 5: 44-45) to pray for those who despitefully use you. I tried to ignore Him. He didn't punish me for not doing it right away. He knew I wanted to be right, but had a hard time reconciling how my ex-husband and all the other men would be punished for the abuses I'd suffered. My honesty with Jesus opened the door for me to be transparent with Him. I reluctantly went about the business of learning to pray for the men who abused me. They were my enemies, but Jesus loved them and commanded that I pray for them. I had to repent for my feelings toward them. I couldn't move forward with my life or with my relationship with Jesus and not love them too.

I started with the deepest most recent pain. I prayed for my ex-husband.

For years I prayed, "Lord bless and keep him in Jesus name, amen." I had nothing else to say.

My prayers changed to, "Lord. I really want to care. I really want to pray for him, but I'm having a hard time. If you really want me to do this, then I'll need your help."

As I prayed for him, I began to see him as a soul that needed saving. The Bible says that he that wins souls is wise. Understanding the need for my soul to be saved, not from hell, my eternal life was secure in Jesus, but from the pain and torment of life, helped me realize maybe his soul needed the same.

Just like my soul, (mind, will and emotions) were damaged and needed saving, his mind, will and emotions needed saving too. Maybe the church killed his spirit. Maybe they killed who God called him to be. Maybe they killed his transparency. Maybe they told him to pretend to be someone he wasn't. Maybe they told him that they wouldn't love him if he wasn't a certain way.

I needed and was looking for love from someone who possibly didn't love himself. How could he love me as Christ loved the church and gave himself for it? He possibly didn't know who he was either. Or maybe he did, but suppressed himself to be accepted by a God the church misrepresented. Perhaps he was a victim, like so many others in the church, of men who improperly taught him how to be a man. Maybe they didn't know how either. Those men were taught by other men about men. Maybe what they said and what they taught didn't line up with God's heart and purpose.

We were better at being friends than spouses for one another. Had I known what I know now, I wouldn't have gotten married at all. I did the right thing for the right reasons at the wrong time and with the wrong person. We didn't have marriage counselors back then to analyze past traumas, relationships, or family histories. No one asked hard questions that required background checks and assessments. If they had, maybe we would've spared each other unnecessary pain.

It's true that love does cover a multitude of faults. Love does and can heal. Love is patient, but love isn't enough if the two people in what should be a love relationship are damaged goods. I can't speak for him. I can only speculate. I know for sure I was damaged goods. The damaged woman I was attracted a man who echoed where I was at the time. He didn't reflect my destiny or God's purpose for my life. The damaged woman I was had no business marrying anyone. I didn't know that at the time.

It was never my fault for being abused in any way. I don't blame myself anymore and never will again. However, there's something to be said for working on myself to never attract the same type of men again. Forgiving him meant freedom from the bondage I was holding myself hostage to.

Me.

I needed to forgive me for holding myself to something for which I had no strength. I was desperately trying to do the right things with the wrong tools, with the wrong people, at the wrong time. In many ways I was the wrong person. I needed to forgive myself for being the wrong person. I needed to forgive myself for not giving myself permission to not be okay. It was really okay not to be okay. I needed to give myself permission to be human and forgive myself for trying to be anything but human. I needed to forgive myself for being flawed.

Siblings

I wanted them to be my siblings. Maybe the desire would not have been so great, if I wasn't in their presence Sunday after Sunday, week after week. After years of wanting, I grew up. I gave up. I asked God to help me forgive them. In doing so, I observed them with more discernment. I was expecting love, acceptance and relationships from people who didn't seem to have it with each other. Maybe they didn't know how to love. Maybe they didn't know how to love me the way I needed to be loved. Maybe it was just as awkward for them back then as it was for me. Maybe their rejection was God's protection. God was in my future while I was stuck in my past and perplexed about my present.

Church

I had to forgive the church for giving misinterpretations of who God is. I had to forgive some in the church for impersonating believers. I had to forgive the church for demanding perfection when Jesus never demanded it. I had to forgive the church for pressuring me to mask my abuses, flaws and pain. I had to forgive the church for protecting the perpetrators of abuse instead of their victims. I had to forgive the church for demanding I quickly forgive without proper instruction or accountability from the perpetrators of the abuses and offenses.

I had to forgive the church for demanding change without love. I had to forgive the church for being impatient with me when they didn't see transformation quick enough.

Pedophile and Rapist

If I'm honest, I can say that I'm still trying to forgive them. Maybe I have already asked in my prayers for help to do it. I'm not sure. It's been years and I still ask God to help me with this. I still ask Him to help me forgive them. I pray about this one until I feel better and then I pray some more about it. When feelings of disgust and disdain overwhelm me about what happened to me, I pray. I cry out to God. I cry until peace replaces anxiety and pain.

LAYERS OF FORGIVENESS

The process of forgiving for me is ongoing. In those times when thoughts and feelings arise, I have to go through prayers of forgiving them again. I have to go through the process of trusting that God hears my heart in the moments I can't verbalize the prayers. It's all a process.

CHAPTER **25**

Surviving Church

AFTER DECADES OF sitting under pastors and leaders who'd fathered children their wives didn't birth, pastors who slept with sheep, pastors who abused their wives, and pastors who pressured people to give money under duress, I was afraid to entrust my soul again. I feared trusting another man called Pastor or Shepherd. If their souls were in trouble, how could they watch over mine? How was I supposed to sit and listen to truth from men who lied?

I thought about the pastor I had when I was ten years old. That pastor allowed the janitor to keep his place in ministry. The pastor allowed him to keep his job at the church. I realized maybe he couldn't correct or fire the janitor because he was compromised. Maybe the janitor knew something about the pastor I didn't know. There could have been secrets that were only secrets to me because the grown folk knew. They knew the pastor had children by a few different women in the church. Maybe that's why he couldn't protect me, because he hadn't protected some of the other sheep either.

I had fear I couldn't push past. I feared not being protected again. I feared leaders who valued the gifted over Godly character and integrity. I feared judgment. I feared misinterpreted scriptures used for the purpose of manipulation and abuse. I feared being vulnerable. I lacked the courage to try again.

I wrote in my journal.

I don't trust pastors and I'm struggling trusting You, Lord. I trust You're real. I trust You to be there for whoever has faith in You. I want to have faith. I want to trust. I just don't, I can't, not with this church thing. Not yet. I fear believing again. What if I'm disappointed again? What if I'm not good enough? I really tried to be good enough. Lord, what if?

I daily shared my concerns with God when I prayed through journaling.

I really don't trust men pastors. Men with power get away everything. How will I ever know if they're safe? What am I supposed to be looking for?

I sensed calmness when I heard Him again.

This time He said, "I know you want to trust Me with this and I'll help you. I was misrepresented by people that thought they were doing the right thing. I'm not them. I'm the head of the church, but I'm not them. No one gets away with anything. I know all and see all. Vengeance is mine. I will repay. You can and will get to, personally and intimately know Me."

For the first time ever, I read (Deuteronomy 22:25-27). I found out through these scriptures that God did care about the abuse I'd suffered. He led me to scriptures to help me identify what a pastor should and shouldn't be. I read in (Jeremiah 3:12-16) that He will give pastors after His own heart. In recent years I came to understand what that really meant. God gives pastors who have His heart. These are pastors who love Him, who chase after Him, and who worship Him in spirit and in truth. These are pastors who consistently study the Word of God and pray for revelation. They understand their assignments and are not distracted by what other churches are doing. They are above reproach, (Titus 1:5-9). These pastors are not perfect men and women. They are human beings with flaws. They have the heart of a shepherd whose focus is leading, teaching and protecting the sheep.

These pastors are faithful husbands and fathers, (1 Timothy 3: 2-12). They love their wives like Jesus Christ loves the church and gave his life for it. These pastors provide for their families. In order for me to live in obedience to God's will, I understood I needed to be part of a local church community. I understood a local fellowship of believers is needed and in accordance to God's word. I needed to be involved in a local faith community because it keeps me grounded and focused. Being in a faith community keeps me connected to people of like faith. The faith community is where I gain strength for my personal journey. The faith community is where I grow in the knowledge of the Word of God. In my local faith community I learned how to study the Word of God and how to be a Kingdom citizen.

There are more judgmental people in faith communities than not. I never wanted to be one of them, and with all of my experiences, I couldn't be. My church survival depends on me keeping a safe distance from pastors and leaders. I need to be close enough to hear God through their Biblical messages, but far from their personalities that can potentially lead to distraction. My church survival depends on me trusting God to lead me in choosing divine connections.

As a woman, so much stress is placed on me, as well as others within church communities. Some church communities can make a woman feel like she can never be worthy enough or holy enough. No little girl grows up with career goals of becoming a whore, a porn star, or a prostitute. Somewhere along the way something happened to her just like something happened to me. The double- edged sword ripped me apart because the abuse I suffered was at the hands of men who said God was using them to protect, cover and teach the way of holiness. Not doing anything to stop the abuse was just as bad as doing it. Making a covenant to love and protect, but instead exposing and abusing was the worse betrayal. I was a wounded woman in rebellion.

Yes, God is Holy, and He commands us to be Holy like Him. But where does it start? How was I or any woman supposed to get to holiness? My heart was shattered to pieces and my life was a reflection of it. Hearing I need to do this and needed to do that or I'm going to hell pushed me farther away from church. Before I could accept rules and abide by them, I needed to be accepted and loved for the mess I was.

I was a woman scorned and didn't want to pretend otherwise. Because I was that woman, my overblown compassion for women who may have suffered like me, drives me to survive church. I needed to survive church for other women who may need someone to look beyond outward appearances. I need to be the one to see the wounded heart and broken soul that's underneath the body that some men lust after.

Remnants of sexual abuse often left me living outside of my body. It was an all too familiar phenomenon. My body and I were regularly at war with one another. I often found myself being an unwilling participant in things I detested. Like many other women, I looked for intimacy and a sense of belonging from men who only wanted to be selfishly pleasured. I know what it's like to look like a sparkling diamond on the outside. I know what it's like to be all made up, with ugly scars on the inside.

When I see the woman with the tight dress, the woman who's overly flirtatious, the woman who chooses to show too much of her body, my heart sinks. I see beyond the surface and wonder who hurt her. Who didn't give her the right attention? Who told her she was nothing more than her body? Who mishandled her? Who abused her? I need to survive church for that woman, because at some point, she's going into a church and will walk to the altar half dressed. She's going to need another woman who understands her. She doesn't need a woman with a title sitting on the front row staring at her in a judgmental kind of way.

At some point, she's not going to be in front of a camera acting out people's fantasies. She's not going to want to pretend anymore that she's enjoying what's really hurting her so people can masturbate. She's going to need help getting out of a lifestyle she got forced into because she was desperate for money to feed her kids or pay the rent. She's going to need someone to survive church so she can come to the church to find love and deliverance. She's going to need someone with whom she can walk out her depression and pain. Walk out all of those things that caused her to go down a path she never meant to go down. She's going to need someone to show her God's heart. So, I need to survive church.

CHAPTER **26**

Somewhere In the Middle

SOMEWHERE IN THE middle is where I sit in my new faith community. The balcony is where I sat when I began my new journey. The balcony was a safe space in the mist of what I still deemed unsafe. The balcony is where I was comfortable. In the balcony were what appeared to be the unchurched, the unmasked, and the uncouth. When I started at my new faith community, in many ways, I was all of these things.

The balcony was my safe space for a little over a year. I did nothing but slip in and out of back doors of the balcony. I only talked with friends who sat with me. It's where I struggled to talk with strangers when the pastor instructed me to do so. No one knew how much anxiety I was feeling trying to be obedient to, "turn and hug someone and tell them…." Hugs hurt. Hugs were unsafe. Hugs led to abuse. It took all the faith I could muster to smile at strangers when I wanted to keep looking straight ahead or down at the floor.

When I prayed about a new faith community, I asked God for a do over. I wanted to forget about everything I knew about church and church people. I wanted to forget about what I thought I knew about Him. I wanted to forget until I learned how to put whatever I knew about the church community and Him in their proper places in my life. Until then, I needed to forget. I wanted to be reintroduced to Jesus. Not the Jesus of legalistic religious organizations, not the Jesus my Grandma and Granddaddy knew, not the Jesus Mama knew, but the Jesus I needed to know.

I came Sunday after Sunday and did nothing but cry. This new faith community was a place where I could cry. It's where I learned to see my hypersensitive self clearly. That's what my therapist said. She said I was hypersensitive, not quite like May Boatwright in, "The Secret Life of Bees," but close. I can easily identify with May. She was super intuitive, observant, and uncontrollably emotional. She felt things deeply, so much so until it became so overwhelming that she felt the need to end her life.

Like her, I feel so deeply until it becomes unbearable sometimes. The frustration of trying to tame my thoughts and emotions can be extremely overwhelming. Things most people brush off can be a challenge for me to do the same. I cry watching sappy movies. I cry when I'm praying for myself or someone else, I cry when I'm angry, when I'm afraid, when I'm happy and when I'm sad. My tears always mean something, and in my new faith community, I was free to explore the why behind my tears. No one watched me while I cried. The people walked around with Kleenex in anticipation of tears. No one judged me when I cried. I was free to learn how to trust Jesus enough for Him to use my tears. Use them for my healing, then maybe for someone else's.

After feeling more comfortable in my new faith community, I slowly moved somewhere in the middle. Not in the balcony, but not in the front either. I was making progress. My foundation was sure enough. My trust in Jesus was growing strong enough. My mind was getting strong enough, just enough for the middle. I'm not sure if I'll ever move to the front. I'm not sure if I'll ever want to. I moved somewhere in the middle of being needy to assisting the needy. I moved somewhere in the middle of faith and fear. I moved somewhere in the middle of working out my own soul salvation with fear and trembling and working in ministry. I moved somewhere between broken and healed. I was somewhere between depressed and happy.

My goal is never the front of the church, but there are good things about the front. The altar is at the front. The front is closer to where the pastor preaches, where the ministers sit, where the music ministry ministers. The front is where people go to receive deliverance and salvation. The front is where people go to get prayer for loved ones. In some ways, people feel closer to God in the front.

The front also has its challenges. Most people who are important, or want to be, move closer to the front. Some pastors and ministers who've been in the way too long are in the front. Nosey people who lack anointing are usually in the front. Some people who forget what God has done for them sit in the front. Some who lack compassion are in the front. Some who are close or think they're close to their leaders are in the front.

The space in the middle works for me. The middle keeps me humbled and compassionate. The middle keeps me close enough to touch God's heart and far enough to reach back and grab someone who's sinking. The middle keeps me balanced. Being broken in the middle keeps me needy for Jesus. I build my altars to God from my middle place. I worship from my middle place. In the middle is where I survive.

CHAPATER **27**

New Life New Eyes

JESUS OCCUPIED MY heart space somewhere between a torn Bible and scripture. It's better than Bible. Not just stories, parables, killings, poetry, history, and prophecy. But it's fulfilment. It's Jesus. The Bible can easily be torn. Stories and parables can be misconstrued. Prophecies of old can be misquoted and their meanings falsified. Poetry can be emotional, but not necessarily life changing. A torn Bible left my soul in a million pieces. Jesus, as the fulfillment of scripture, continually saves and gives me life principles to live by, piecing my soul back together.

Getting to know God's heart and personality through Jesus guides my daily walk. Studying His life through the gospels; how He lived, how He interacted with people, how he treated his friends, what angers Him and what makes Him happy teaches me how to live my life. These examples teach me how to have relationships. His command to love God and love people simplifies my life.

All of the ways I sought to find Him and His love in religious communities, I hadn't realized my own family was the perfect epitome of Him and His love. God's perfect love was manifested in the way Granddaddy cared for Grandma, the way he spoke up for her, talked with her, protected her, got her off the white man's land and built her homes to live in. God's love was manifested in the way Granddaddy took care of his children and grandchildren. Something simple as my favorite cereal would be my greatest example of love shown to me by my Granddaddy.

The command Jesus gave to love God and love people just as I loved myself manifested within my family and sister friends. The tradition of family reunions my grandparents and great aunts and uncles started when I was ten and continues to now, is a testament to love in action. It's in the way my family never ends a reunion without a worship service honoring and giving praise to God for His unfailing grace to all of us. God's love was manifested in my family without the complication of legalism, over emphasis on spiritual gifts and titles.

I'd come full circle to realize what I was looking for I already had. I had God and His love within my own family and my sister friends. I had people who God showed His love through, near and far. They were there in the many times I thought I didn't have love because it wasn't coming from my biological dad, his family and men. I was so overtaken with loss and horrific abuse I didn't notice God and His love was always surrounding me.

I spent the majority of my life striving for love and acceptance from God. I accepted His love for me when I took Him at His Word to trust Him. I received His love when I asked Him to allow me to feel His love in my soul. He answered by an unspeakable embrace that I'd never felt before, and one that I'll always pursue for the rest of my life. I started saying to myself what He said to me. "I love you, Sharon. I really love you, Sharon. There is nothing you can do or not do to make me stop loving you."

I stood in the mirror and said, "God loves me. God loves me. God loves me." I said it over and over again, day in and day out until I believed it in my heart. I said it until nothing or no one could make me believe otherwise.

Seeing God as Father gave me identity. Trusting God as Father released me from the pressure of toiling. I didn't have to worry. I didn't have to fret. I didn't have to earn anything from Him. Trusting meant automatically receiving everything I need from my Father. I was His child because I believed in Him. I was His child because He said I was. I believe Him through faith in Jesus Christ. He's my Daddy "Abba Father" and I'm His daughter. I now have an intimate relationship with Him. I didn't have to mull over it in my head.

Like a child to a daddy, you don't think about if Daddy's going to feed you, clothe you, shelter you or protect you. You just know he will. I was finally at that point. I was at the point of just knowing. Now I had hope for my future. Now I have confidence in Him to accomplish anything. If He didn't do whatever He had a good reason. His reason was and is me. His reason for doing and/or not doing for me has everything to do with me and what He knows is best for me. It's me living in Him. It's me in His purpose for my life. It took years to realize it and as a result let Justin go in my heart. It's me and Him walking through this journey called life together.

All of my life I waited for Him to show up in my heart and love me. I was waiting for Him to love me in speaking in tongues. I was waiting for Him to love me in the clothes I was instructed to wear. I was waiting for Him to love me in a Pentecostal dance. I was waiting for Him to love me through religious communities who said they knew and loved Him. I needed God to tell me I was a good woman. I needed Him to tell me I wasn't a whore, a bitch, or hard to get along with. I needed Him to tell me I wasn't crazy. I needed Him to tell me living with mental illness, being a product of an affair, being a battered woman, being a sexually abused woman, being butt, breasts and thighs was not all there was to me.

The revelation of God and His love for me didn't come in religious practices. It didn't come with ignoring His grace through legalism. There were no lighting strikes, no loud voices of thunder. He was just there. He already loved me when I didn't recognize love.

God was in the memory of Grandma and Granddaddy.

God was in my family gatherings and reunions.

God was in the many times my sister friends and I get together for meals, talks, and laughter.

God was in the colors of fall and in the warm cups of Starbucks mocha coffee on crisp nights I so enjoy.

God was in the poetry and short stories I wrote. While I was writing, He was writing my story over. Through each word written, through therapists, through medications, through Mama, Gina, Jeremy, my Uncle Daddy, aunties, uncles and cousins, I was getting a new story. I was getting a do over. I was getting a new life. I was beginning to see new things with new eyes. I got answered prayers.

The fog was lifted. The scales were off. I analyzed my church experiences. I observed through the study of scriptures, and compared them to what I saw and experienced in some church communities. There was a clear disconnect. It became clear to me the church as I knew it, took on the mentality and actions of the Pharisees and Sadducees, rather than the disciples of Jesus. Because the disciples had been with Jesus, they knew His heart and took on his characteristics. They believed and obeyed Him. As a result, they were able to turn their world upside down. They were able to effectively teach others how to be disciples.

The Pharisees and Sadducees were more concerned about outward appearances, laws, and governing. They were more concerned with status and position rather than love and care. They talked about the laws of Moses, about Jesus' coming and His grace. But, they didn't recognize love and grace in action. They didn't recognized Jesus, even when He was among them.

I saw myself clearly. With no fault of my own, I allowed my abuses and mental challenges to own me. Not because I wanted to, but because I didn't know how not to. I organized and lived my life around depression and abuse. I fit college and career around futile moments of pleasure. I scheduled around lots of insomnia, sleepiness, overeating and undereating.

My best sister friend didn't know she'd started small revolts of disruption in my life. She didn't know she was helping me carve out a life worth living. I painstakingly went along with her nudging and pushing me out of my comfort zones, no matter how self-destructive they were. I thanked God for her every day. I thanked God she ignored and sometimes endured me kicking and screaming by way of bad attitudes, huffs and puffs. I didn't know then that freedom and deliverance took work, lots of work.

I couldn't take back my life as I knew it. I couldn't get back relationships I'd lost, nor did I want to. I didn't know I didn't want those relationships back until I got a new life and new eyes. The moment I understood that mental illness was no more my fault than the abuses I'd suffered, is the moment I saw my life differently. There was nothing I did wrong to deserve any of it. There was nothing I could've done differently to avoid it. There is absolutely nothing wrong with me.

I owe it to myself to know myself at every stage of my life. I'm learning how to check on me, slow down and rest when needed. I'm free from people's opinions of me. I understand that just because someone else can do it doesn't mean I can and that's okay. I often look at the emotional mess that falls in my lap or I sometimes pick up. I untangle my thoughts, pick up the feelings I dropped along the way and try again tomorrow.

I learned to sing again. I put aside songs my Grandma sang or songs that helped Mama along. Instead I started singing songs that helped me when I got scared. I started singing songs that helped when doubts of His love for me tried to creep in. I sang and listened to songs that spoke to the sentiments of my heart. Songs of worship became my air and breath. Worship lyrics said what I so often couldn't say.

I often think about Grandma and Granddaddy. They didn't have "Pentecost" or "religion" to pass down, but what they passed down was something much more valuable. They passed down their faith in Jesus Christ, their faith and love for family, their respect and love for each other, their example of how men should treat women and how women should honor men worthy of that honor, a spirit of giving and a strong responsibility to fight for justice. It got them through the many horrendous stages of life's struggles and racism. They had no idea that all they'd passed down would reach all the way to me and would end up saving my life.

I've come full circle since I was that little girl in New Orleans, Louisiana and Chicago, Illinois. I've circled right back to my ancestors and the generations that followed them, to my strength, to my life and to my God, Jesus Christ.

References

Monk-Kidd, Sue. *The Secret Life of Bees*. New York: Penguin Books, 2003

www.ingramcontent.com/pod-product-compliance
Lightning Source LLC
Chambersburg PA
CBHW070937180426
43192CB00039B/2309